A Tribute To Bishop King

TODAY is the anniversary of the death of [illegible] who was Bishop of [illegible] from [illegible] wh[illegible]

THE MIND AND WORK OF BISHOP KING

ACKNOWLEDGEMENTS

Our thanks are due to the Author (the Right Hon. G. W. E. Russell) and to the Publishers (Messrs. Smith, Elder & Co.) for their kindness in allowing us to make use of, and to quote certain passages from, *Edward King, Bishop of Lincoln.*

We desire also to express our obligations to Messrs. Longmans, Green & Co. for a few quotations from *The Love and Wisdom of God*, and from Bishop King's *Sermons and Addresses.*

B. W. R.
J. W. T.

J. L. Cooper
Fr. J. A. Downes
Mar: 9. 1918.

The Bishop (June, 1906).

(From a photo by Harrison, Lincoln.)

Frontispiece.

The Mind and Work of Bishop King

BY

B. W. RANDOLPH

Canon of Ely, formerly Principal of Ely Theological College

AND

J. W. TOWNROE

Vicar of St. Peter-at-Gowts, and Canon of Lincoln

WITH PREFACE BY THE BISHOP OF LONDON

Thy gentleness hath made me great.—*Ps.* xviii. 35.

A. R. MOWBRAY & CO. LTD.
LONDON: 28 Margaret Street, Oxford Circus, W. 1
OXFORD: 9 High Street
MILWAUKEE, U.S.A.: The Young Churchman Co.

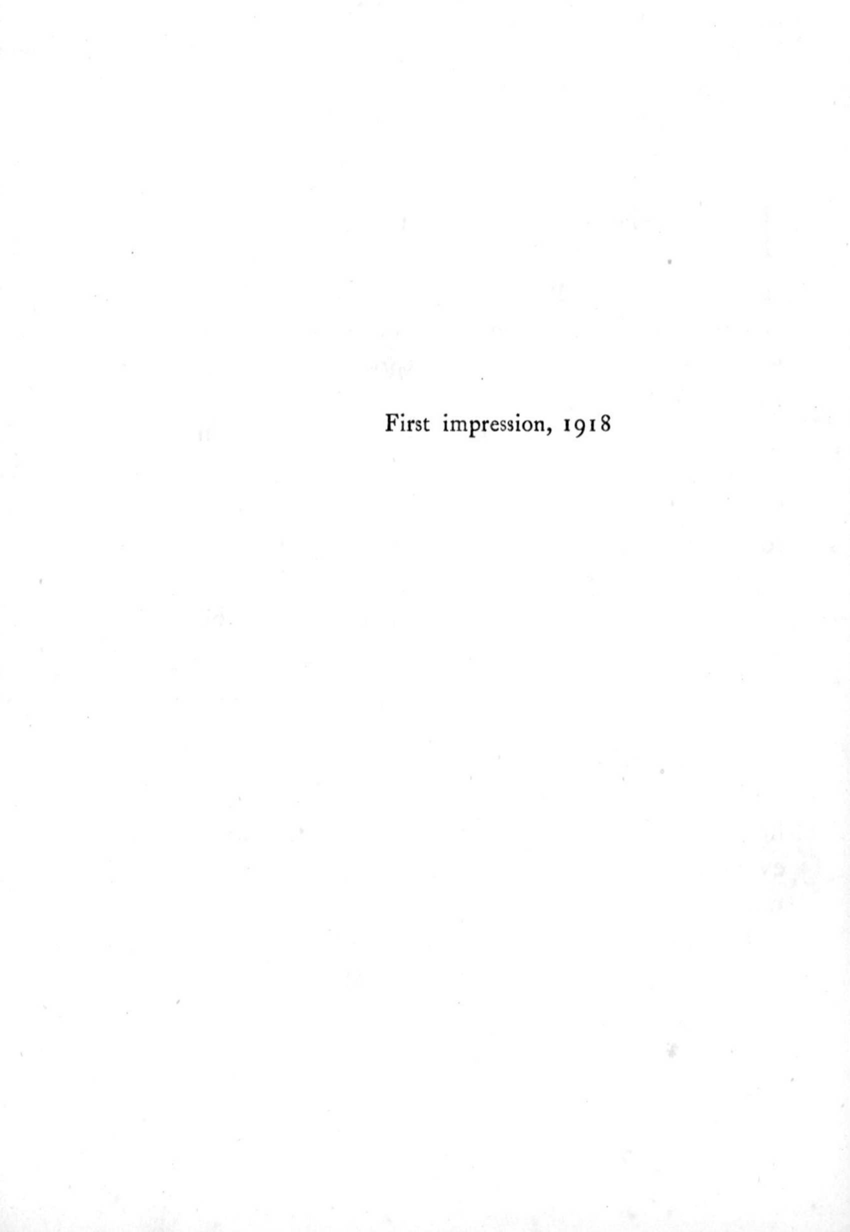

First impression, 1918

PREFACE

IT is a very congenial task during a few days of Christmas holiday to sit down and write, as requested, a Preface on the Feast of the Apostle of Love to another book about one who was pre-eminently an "Apostle of Love" to our generation.

We were all very grateful to Mr. Russell for his excellent Life of our friend and saint, but I am glad to know that another book is to be sent out, of which the first chapter has been sent me as a specimen, and if the rest of the chapters are as good as the first it will be a delightful book.

For indeed we cannot have another Edward King, and we must make the most of the one we were given, as a gift from heaven. I will not attempt to anticipate what the reader will find so well expressed in the first chapter, with every word of which I am in complete agreement.

But perhaps I may illustrate what will be found there by a few personal experiences of the man, as I knew him. I first saw him when I "sat under him," as Pastoral Professor at Oxford, and it only came out afterwards that the largish fee for instructing us how to read in public was paid by the Pastoral Professor.

Years passed, and I saw nothing of him until, in passing through Oxford in 1884, I heard him speak about the Oxford House, little thinking I should have any connection with it, and he warned a little gathering he was addressing not to go there *instead of* a Theological College, but *beforehand*—a warning which I saw carried out in numberless cases in the nine years during which I was subsequently head of that institution; but the really famous story in connection with the Oxford House was his "Rub Lightly" address, which I did not hear.

He was on his way to Lincoln, and everything had gone except a solitary match-box, on which the words "Rub Lightly," as we all know, are often written; this he gave as the key-note of the new adventure, and every one who has ever worked in such a district as Bethnal Green knows that no better advice could be given.

It was not until I became Bishop of London that I really got to know intimately one who rapidly became my father and friend. His loving-kindness and tender care was shown to younger bishops as well as to the people of his old diocese, and often did he honour me by staying with me at Fulham or at London House.

His great love of horses, mentioned in the first chapter, was well known to me, and I sent him and his great friend, Bishop Paget, from St. Paul's to Fulham behind a spanking pair of cobs, which I then had, drawing a light victoria. I told the coachman to drive them down the Embankment all the way, and they did the distance in seventeen minutes. For some reason I had to be at Fulham that day, and was not at the service; but the bishop sprang from the carriage when I went out to meet him with both hands outstretched: "Oh! it was glorious, dear friend; I did enjoy it; and think! we *might have had bronchitis!*"—a thanksgiving which Bishop Paget paralleled next day after we two had had a vigorous game of lawn tennis: "I did enjoy that game, bishop; think, *we might have been fat!*"

Every night I used to lead Bishop King home to London House from the House of Lords during the long debates on the first

Education Bill; and he had such touching confidence that, when with his increasing deafness he was doubtful about the very complicated details on which we were voting and rapidly dividing, he said: "I always follow you into the lobby, bishop, when I am in doubt"—a compliment which I deeply appreciated.

One speaks of this lighter side of our friendship, because it would be telling "God's secrets" to tell of the great spiritual help he was to me as a bishop, both by his counsel and even more by his example. When you want to be like Jesus Christ in all the complicated details of a bishop's life it is an enormous help to have an example before your eyes of one who more completely represents "the attractiveness of goodness" than any one else you had ever met.

This help Bishop King gave to me, and I have no doubt to thousands of others; but as one humble member of those thousands I am pleased to have been allowed to lay this little tribute at his feet.

A. F. LONDON.

BOURNEMOUTH:
Feast of St. John the Evangelist,
1917.

Dr. King and the Bishop of London (June, 1907).

(From a photo by Harrison, Lincoln.)

Page viii.

CONTENTS

LIST OF ILLUSTRATIONS

THE MIND AND WORK OF BISHOP KING

CHAPTER I

EDWARD KING

Ben parve messo e famigliar di Cristo.
Par. xii. 73.

Messenger he seemed and friend
Fast knit to Christ.
Cary.

CHAPTER I

EDWARD KING

THIS volume is not a biography, at least not in the ordinary acceptance of that term. It is but little concerned with chronology, it aims rather at being a portrait, or at least a sketch, of one of the most remarkable spiritual leaders of the last half of the nineteenth century. Here was a man who, during the fifty-six years of his ordained life, exercised from first to last a strangely powerful influence on those with whom he came in contact; and his influence was always of the best and highest kind. It never seemed to fail—as curate in a country parish, as principal of a theological college, as a university professor, and, finally, for five-and-twenty years, as a bishop.

Wherever he went spiritual power went with him, and radiated out from him to a remarkable degree. Men and women felt themselves drawn up to a higher level, if not of attainment, at least of aspiration.

"We have buried our saint," wrote one, after

attending Bishop King's funeral,[1] "and his beautiful face will never be seen by us on earth again, nor his winning, playful smile; and to many of us who have loved him so much and so long this world will be much poorer.

"This is what was felt by every soul who had seen and known Edward King.

"To die in the middle of his people, without an enemy in the world; to have a great multitude silently tearful round him as his body was borne up his great cathedral; to have won by his simple, unflinching life of faithful witness the undying love of thousands and the deep respect of all, and, as Browning says of Pheidippides—

> 'Never decline, but gloriously as he began,
> So to end gloriously'—

"that was the halo of our saint's death."

So his friends thought of him.

You cannot "analyse the sunset," but it is inevitable that future generations will ask what sort of man this was in his public words and acts, in his mind and work, in his inner life, amongst those who knew him best. What can you tell us about him? How was

[1] Bishop (Ingram) of London.

it all done? What was he like, this last immediate disciple of the Tractarians?

Was he a sort of latter-day Bishop Andrewes? How did he hand on the doctrinal tradition of Pusey, Keble, and Isaac Williams? How did he carry on the saintly tradition of George Herbert, Bishop Ken, and Bishop Wilson?

This volume is an attempt, however inadequate, to answer such questions, and to leave a record for "those that come after," that those who knew not Edward King in the flesh may yet thank God for the gift that He gave in him to the English Church.

Everybody knows that he was a strong Churchman. He was immovable in his conviction that the English Church is an integral portion of the great Catholic Church of Christ. He believed with his whole heart that in the convulsions of the sixteenth century the English Church had been guided and overruled by Providence to retain the valid succession of the Episcopate, and with that, and because of it, the due administration of the Catholic Sacraments. He believed that the English Church, which he loved with a whole-hearted filial devotion, had been preserved through the perils of the Reformation by the providential guidance of God; and that, though she had suffered in the stress and strain of the storm, yet that she had lost nothing of what was necessary to her Catholic life and witness, and that she was entirely justified in her repudiation of the excessive claims of Rome.[1] He was a strong Churchman, and his great desire in administering his diocese was, as he would often say, to get the piety of the people on to Church lines, in order that, learning to value the Sacraments more and more, they might be brought into closer touch with GOD through Jesus Christ, and lead holier, happier, and brighter lives.

But he was much more than a strong Churchman; he was a great lover of souls.

No one loved men in their troubles and sorrows, in their trials and temptations more than Edward King did. No one was more tender and gentle with his penitents (and he heard many confessions), no one more sensitive

[1] "Though we would grant to the See of Rome her ancient primacy, yet we cannot accept it as it is now offered, transformed into a *quasi*-sacramental Headship."—*Primary Charge, 1886*, p. 25.

to the sorrows of others. Yet he was a man of unconquerable hopefulness. He never lost touch with the young; his heart remained young to the last, and he was always ready to look on the bright side of things. Hence his inexhaustible cheerfulness and buoyancy. He never, in Sydney Smith's phrase, "added paralysis to piety," but was, to the end, full of the joy of living, and thus able to inspire others in such a marked degree.

His very presence was an inspiration; one always felt better for having seen him, and better able to face life. He cheered you and encouraged you, and would send you away from a visit to Lincoln ready to begin again and to go bravely on; while the vision of his radiant and joyous face as he stood at the Old Palace door to see you off kept dancing before your eyes on your way home. Love, joy, sympathy, humour, hope—all these gifts and graces of the Spirit were in Edward King to a marked degree, and made him the spiritual genius that he was. Few things daunted him. Difficult people he would sometimes describe as "trials"; and once he said, many years ago (before he was a bishop) of a very troublesome and difficult person, "I don't always feel certain, dear friend, that ——— will get to Paradise ; but I am sure she ought to be a great help in getting *us* there ! "

" Serve the Lord *with gladness* " might have served as his motto through life—as the motto of good Bishop Hacket ; and he would often preach from St. John's words, " His commandments are not grievous."

Yet he was under no illusions as to the strain and burden of life. In later years he would not infrequently say, "Life needs steady courage."

Though few men appreciated more fully the joy and gladness of family life, yet he himself lived a solitary life, and knew the strain which that means to an affectionate and sympathetic nature. To the last he was a soldier on a campaign ; there was in him, as Dr. Holland said, " the spirit of an old war-horse."

" God has not given me a *chin* for nothing," he once said playfully as he insisted on going through with some little difficult job.

His great strength lay in his power of love, love disciplined and controlled, but of wonderful power. Few men have had the pastoral instinct and the pastoral heart in such a high degree. It was a true indication of his character when he had the words of St. Paul carved over the doorway of the Old Palace at Lincoln "*Pascite Gregem.*" And if it be asked what was the secret of his power, what made him such a unique personality, able to charm every one with whom he came in contact, from a duke to a ploughboy, from a duchess to a kitchen-maid?—what was it that won and fascinated them and made them instinctively trust him—old and young alike—first at Wheatley or at Cuddesdon, at Oxford, and then in Lincolnshire? —if it be asked what the secret was, the answer seems to be that it was the power of sympathy linked with a special gift of natural attractiveness, together with the fact that he had real spiritual insight and understood the needs of the soul. There was that beautiful, kindly, *luminous* face that you were obliged to look at if you were near it. You did not ask whether he was "handsome" or "good-looking," you simply thought or said "What a beautiful face!" And then, if you heard him talking, or if he spoke to you, you realized at once that it was not merely physical beauty which had drawn you to him. There was a singular beauty of character, of which the face was the outward and visible sign; and the most obvious, overwhelming, persistent trait of this beautiful character was its sympathy. You felt that he instinctively entered into your special case and your special interests.

"What are you doing?" said the bishop at a friend's house to a little girl as she came downstairs on Sunday morning.

"Learning my collect," was the answer.

"Isn't it a horrid long one?" said the bishop.

And the little girl ran to her mother in the greatest delight, "O mother, I think the bishop must be an archangel."

What had raised him in the child's mind to the angelic hierarchy? The power of sympathy. Instinctively he had entered into the child's point of view. It *was* a long collect.

"The bishop's a wonderful man," said a stable-lad after his Confirmation. "He must have been a stable-boy himself; he knows all about us."

Next to his sympathy and love of souls, perhaps we should put his gift of wisdom. He always had his affections well in hand, and he was anything but a narrow ecclesiastic; rather he was, in the true sense of the words, a broad-minded man with a very shrewd judgement. He would give very sound and good advice on many subjects which might have no bearing at all on ecclesiastical matters. He possessed a gift of sanctified common sense and worldly wisdom which was apt to surprise those who only knew him at a distance. The secret of it was partly, no doubt, that he had been accustomed to mix with all kinds of people in his home life in early days ; but also that he had a special gift of wisdom — that wisdom which is from above, and which is "pure, peaceable, gentle, easy to be intreated, full of mercy and good fruits, without partiality, and without hypocrisy."

In trying to sum up his character, his love of nature must not be forgotten. All nature was to him a burning bush aflame with God —and how he loved the spring and summer months !

"I still love birds and flowers," he wrote towards the end of his life, and it was a joy to him in his old age to sit at his study window and watch the birds on the lawn, and speak of the "marvellous creation of a bird's nest." All nature spoke to him of God ; and, without any very deep knowledge of botany, he loved plants and flowers. The buds coming out on the hedges, the leaves on the trees, the eggs in the birds' nests—all these and many like familiar phenomena of country life were laid under contribution to illustrate his Confirmation addresses and his sermons in the country parishes. Alive and alert to all around him, he felt in sympathy and harmony with nature, and in league with the beasts of the field.

"Every springtime shows us a resurrection after the apparent death of winter—the trees and flowers were 'not dead but sleeping.' It is a constant miracle of wonder and delight to me to watch through the early days of spring the still, dark, and dead-like stems of the trees in our orchards. It seems so unlikely that the dark, dull stem should ever be the channel for a life of beauty and of self-production. Inch after inch, as the eye rises from the ground, there seems no hope of any future glory ; and yet, when the appointed time has come, we see the miracle of its organic life performed, and blossom after blossom is unfolded, and then the full fruit is formed." [1]

In a sermon preached not long before the end of his life there is another glimpse of his intense love of Nature :—

[1] *The Love and Wisdom of God*, p. 334. (Longmans.)

"I will thank Him for the pleasures given me through my senses, for the glory of the thunder, for the mystery of music, the singing of birds, and the laughter of children. I will thank Him for the pleasures of seeing, for the delights through colour, for the awe of the sunset, the beauty of flowers, the smile of friendship, and the look of love; for the changing beauty of the clouds, for the wild roses in the hedges, for the form and beauty of birds . . . for the sweetness of flowers and the scent of hay-time. O Lord, the earth is full of Thy riches."[1]

He had no small share of that gaiety and gladness which we are apt to associate specially with such saints as St. Francis of Assisi, and he shared with them their love of plants and birds and beasts. The greater part of his life he had spent in the country, and his love for it increased rather than diminished as the years passed. Ever since Wheatley days, when he used to go for long walks and take immense interest in teaching the village boys

[1] From a sermon preached in Lincoln Cathedral at the Thanksgiving for the cessation of the typhoid epidemic in the city, June, 1905. See *Sermons and Addresses*, p. 37. (Longmans.)

about plants and flowers, he loved the country; and perhaps it was when worshipping in a village church that he felt specially near to God.

Another mark of his character was gentleness. Through and through he felt how gentle God is in His dealings with us, and, for all his strength of character, Bishop King was one of the gentlest of men. Gentleness is not weakness, but restrained strength; and you felt that he had himself well in hand, that he had well disciplined that strong affectionate heart and that burning zeal, and this discipline showed itself in self-restraint and gentleness. He believed in the power of gentleness to bring out the best that is in a man. He may have been deceived now and again in taking too kindly an estimate of this or that individual; but he would have said that it was better so than to give way to roughness and harshness.

"It is better to be over-charitable than over-strict," he writes in one of his letters.

He had, like other men, *les défauts de ses qualités*; and his archdeacons might sometimes have felt that his tender heart was a little too much the ruler now and then when they would have had him deal more drastically with a lazy or criminous clerk. They might not have said that the bishop was an ideal disciplinarian. For the same reasoning his examining chaplains did not find it easy to persuade him to reject an ordination candidate on the ground of insufficiency of knowledge, if the bishop was fully persuaded of his goodness and piety and the reality of his vocation. There was in him too, perhaps, a tendency sometimes to attribute goodness to people in a higher degree than facts seemed to warrant.

But he had in general a very shrewd insight into human character. People in all ranks of life—cabmen, railwaymen, servants, shop-assistants, farm hands and ploughboys, laymen of all ranks, not to speak of clergy and Ordination candidates, nor the multitudes of undergraduates who came under his influence in earlier days—all these could testify to his gentleness and kindness. He was a living illustration of the beatitude that "the meek shall inherit the earth." He never pushed his way anywhere, yet he inevitably became the centre of any group of people in which he might find himself; he went through the world in a singularly gentle way. One of his favourite texts from which he would often preach was "Thy gentleness hath made me great."

Closely allied to his gentleness was his love of peace and concord. He was a striking example of how possible it is, if a man has the Spirit of Christ, to be quite true to one's own convictions (unwelcome though some of them may be to others) and yet to live in absolute peace and concord with those who differ from us. After all, men everywhere respect consistency; and consistency of character, when it goes hand-in-hand with love and sympathy and gentleness, evokes not merely respect, but affection and loyalty.

But, above all, he had a heart brimming over with love to God and love to man. "King is a royal fellow," was said of him at Oxford, and this "royalty" remained with him all through life. It was the "royalty" of a life lived close to God, in friendship and loving communion with God, in seeing God in everything, and specially in every soul with whom he came in contact. And, loving God, he loved to bring other souls into communion with God, that they too might have the consciousness of His presence and His love. This explains all that he did or said or was. He was not a great administrator or disciplinarian. But in point of moral beauty and pastoral zeal he came very near to the ideal bishop. His name should go down to posterity as that of one who realized, as few have done, what the pastoral side of a bishop's life ought to be; and that means primarily that, loving God, he sought to bring others to the love of God.

Did he value the Church and the Sacraments?—it was because he saw in them the divinely-ordered means of bringing men to love God, and to love one another in God. Did he lay store on the dignity of outward worship, and long for a more free and generous expression of it?—it was because he knew that men are taught by the eye as well as by the ear, and that many hearts are uplifted to the love of God by the outward expression of beauty of worship.

Did he value and love his Confirmations? —it was because he felt himself at such times in direct touch with the young whom he longed to bring nearer to God.

Did he never refuse simple entertainments to which he was invited?—they were opportunities in the unshackled freedom of social intercourse, indirectly or directly, of leading others to the knowledge and love of God.

That, surely, was the constant refrain and burden of his preaching, and the underlying principle of his life—to bring others nearer to God, and, in God, to one another. All his brightness and gaiety, all the charm and fascination of his personality, all his attractive and winning ways, all his uplifting cheerfulness, all his strong helpfulness, all his old-fashioned and delightful courtesy, all his gifts and graces were devoted to this end—to bring others to love God, and, in God, to love one another.

Perhaps the main lesson of his life could hardly be summed better than by the words of St. John, which are carved on his monument in the south transept of the cathedral :—

"Beloved, let us love one another, for love is of God, and every one that loveth is born of God and knoweth God."

CHAPTER II

EARLY LIFE

L'animo, ch' è creato ad amar presto,
Ad ogni cosa è mobile che piace,
Tosto che dal piacere in atto è desto.

Purg. xviii. 19–21.

The soul, created apt
To love, moves versatile which way soe'er
Aught pleasing prompts her, soon as she is waked
By pleasure into act.

Cary.

CHAPTER II

EARLY LIFE

EDWARD King came of a clerical family, for his grandfather, Walker King, had been Bishop of Rochester—he died two years before Edward was born—and his father was Walker King, Canon and Archdeacon of Rochester, and Rector of Stone in Kent. Archdeacon King had married, in 1823, Anne Heberden, daughter of William Heberden, M.D. There were ten children of the mar-tiage, Edward being the third child and second son.

He was born in London on December 29, 1829, privately baptized on January 4, 1830, and afterwards received into the Church at Stone. Edward's mother, Mrs. King, was an exceedingly attractive and beautiful character, so that the home life at Stone left an indelible impression on his mind. "Our English homes may be said to be the Castles of England, and family religion the Keep of the Castle," he wrote in later life.

The younger brothers and sisters were kept somewhat rigidly to the schoolroom and nursery, but with his sister Anne it was different; she was an invalid for twelve years, and Edward sometimes used to spend the whole night by her bedside. He learnt Italian in order that he might share her love of Dante; from her he derived his interest in botany; and in his constant attendance on her he developed that tactful, sympathetic, and unfussy manner in visiting invalids which always marked his ministry. He was even in his boyhood considered, it is said, "the good one of the family." "We were never so happy," writes one of his sisters, "as when we were all together, owing greatly, I think, to the love and sympathy our parents had for us all." Being rather delicate as a boy he was not sent to any school, but was taught daily by the Curate of Stone, the Rev. John Day, who subsequently became Vicar of Ellesmere in Shropshire. Hither Edward King accompanied him, and used to help in the choir and to conduct a Bible Class for men.

In February, 1848, Edward went up to Oxford, and was entered at Oriel College, where his elder brother Walker was already

Edward King and his elder brother, Walker King, in childhood.

(From a crayon sketch.)

Page 22.

an undergraduate. Here he came under the influence of the Rev. Charles Marriott, Fellow and Tutor of the college, who was closely identified with the Tractarian Movement, being an intimate friend and disciple of Dr. Pusey. In later life King used not infrequently to speak of Charles Marriott, and always in the highest terms, as one whose "noble life was a living commentary on the Four Gospels;" adding—"If I have any good in me I owe it to Charles Marriott."

King took little part in the athletic side of university life; he was fond of riding and an excellent horseman, but it appears his chief recreation was walking, and, in a lesser degree, boating.

He was held in the highest respect by all his contemporaries. He was strict in his life, observing the fasts of the Church by absenting himself from the college hall on those days, and being extremely regular in his attendance at chapel. This latter habit was the occasion of a remark made to King by Hawkins, the somewhat severe Provost of Oriel. At one of the reviews of work held at the end of each term, called "Collections," the Provost noticed Edward King's record of attendance at the college chapel, and, looking at him, said, "I observe, Mr. King, that you have not missed a single chapel during the term. I must warn you, Mr. King, that even a regular attendance at chapel *may* degenerate into formalism."

There is another story told of King's life at Oxford (which may or may not be accurate), viz. that he once went to a "wine" in the college, but when one of the company began to sing a bad song, King immediately left the room, and, it is said, never went to a "wine" again.

His health as a young man, and indeed until he reached middle life, was never very good, so that he did not read for Honours, but took an ordinary degree in 1851. The following year he went on a tour to the Holy Land.

On the first page of the diary which he kept during this tour there is the following entry :—

"Lyons, Hôtel de l'Univers, February 6th, 8 p.m.—The feelings with which one leaves one's home to wander on the continent for any length of time cannot be understood but by those who have experienced them, and by those they will never be forgotten."

Opposite to this entry the following touching

remarks have been entered in his own handwriting :—

"Quite true, February 3, 1897, i.e. after having been preserved with such exceeding mercy and goodness for forty-five years, how thankful and trustful one ought to be !"

And again :

"Yes, this is true more and more, now I am seventy ; February 3, 1900. *Deo gratias.*"

And finally, just a month before his death, he writes, now in a very shaky hand :—

"Yes, again, this is true more and more, now I am eighty. February 3, 1910. Verily His mercy endureth for ever. *Deo gratias.*"

These entries show what a profound impression this tour to the Holy Land made upon him ; and in his old age, writing to a friend who was contemplating a similar pilgrimage, he says : "It is fifty-five years since I was in the Holy Land, and my visit is still a source of comfort and pleasure to me."

In speaking in later life of this tour he used sometimes to say that when he reached the sacred places he felt that one great impression made upon his mind was that "our Blessed LORD is not here now *as* He once was. He has been here, He has trod on this earth, His human eyes have looked on all this; but He Himself is now to be sought for in the spiritual world. He is still 'very Man and very God' but 'He is not here, He is risen.'"

From this diary it appears that the party landed at Beyrout, and went on horseback down the coast past Tyre and Sidon and Acre into Palestine itself. Jerusalem was visited, and a stay of some days was made there, with excursions to the Jordan and the Dead Sea.

The return journey was made through the Holy Land by way of the plain of Esdraelon to Nazareth and Galilee, and eventually the travellers reached Damascus, where the journal suddenly breaks off. King returned to England in June, having been away from home for some five months.

The diary is for the most part an observant and intelligent chronicle of the tour, but there is little in it that calls for special comment. Two extracts, however, may be permitted. The first is his entry on crossing the Channel from Folkestone to Boulogne:—

"Feb. 4, 1852.—We went on board the boat at 8.45 a.m. It was raining and blowing. There were fifteen horses on board, which, as

Edward King.

(From a crayon drawing by G. Drummond, 1855, *by permission of Rev. Dr. Brightman.)*

Page 26.

we expected, added greatly to the rolling of the boat; and soon my vain hopes in the powers of saffron—which, according to Mr. Day's advice, I had procured in a bag—began to vanish. At first I stood and talked loud and quick, but soon sat down on a camp-stool and underwent all the horrors of anticipation for about an hour, when the stern reality was no longer to be denied, and I suffered most miserably."

The other, dated March 26th, when he and his party were riding down the coast of Syria. He is describing some untoward experiences which they suffered while encamping in a small village in the plain of Acre, and he notes :—

"This was one of those useful days for the exercise of patience only to be found in travelling."

On his return to England, King acted for a short time, during 1853, as tutor to Lord Lothian's brothers; and on Trinity Sunday in the following year he was ordained deacon at Cuddesdon by Bishop Wilberforce, and priest in 1855. His first and only curacy was at Wheatley, a village five miles from Oxford, and a mile and a half from Cuddesdon. The vicar was the Rev. Edward Elton, to whom King had been recommended by the bishop as "a gentleman and a Christian."

Wheatley, like many another village, was a rough place in those days, and it was in dealing with boys and lads in this parish that King first manifested those very remarkable powers of influence over men and lads which were such a marked feature of his later ministry. He interested them in botany, he superintended a night school in the winter months. This kind of work was thoroughly congenial to him, and to the end of his life his love for village life in general, and for Wheatley in particular, never left him. He used to go for long walks, and take immense interest in teaching the children about flowers and plants and birds.

One who was a boy at Wheatley at this time, and who only passed away recently, remembered him coming into the school-room, and asking the master whether he might take Charles —— out for a walk : "He took me up to his room," he wrote, "and gave me some plums before we went out." This boy, under King's guidance, became first a pupil-teacher, then a student at Culham, and finally a schoolmaster. He had a complete set of letters from King, the first of which was dated 1857, and the last 1909, without the omission of a single year. The first eighteen of the bishop's published *Spiritual Letters* were addressed to this almost life-long friend. This unremitting correspondence illustrates King's care not to drop people, a habit against which he often used to warn young men in later life. The following quotations are made to illustrate his continued recollection of and love for Wheatley.

From Cuddesdon, in 1871, he writes :—

"I have been obliged, these last few years, to spend the best part of my time in reading ; but if I should be free from the college I should go on in a parish just as we used to at Wheatley. That was a simple, unworldly, affectionate life, and that is what we want. I do not think people are simple enough in their religious relations. I wish we could be more open and united in the use of the churches as houses of prayer and praise. . . .

"The simple carter lads require to be surrounded with a constant flame of love to save them from the hardness which their life with the animals and rough men brings on them. Our dear country poor—I feel more suited to them than others—require to be helped one by one ; they are very ignorant, have very little time, work very hard, and often with poor food ; they require a great deal of loving, watchful sympathy."

From Lincoln, in 1895, he writes :—

"It seems only yesterday that you used to come down to my room with dear G. and J., and we used to sit and talk together. I don't know that I have ever been happier. I ought to be very thankful for all God's goodness to me. I did not think that I should live so long. I think our way of looking at things was the right one, we saw where true happiness was to be found. I long to promote the same kind of spirit in our country parishes. The Lincolnshire people are very nice, strong-headed, deep-hearted people ; my happiest time is when I am confirming in the country parishes ; that I enjoy immensely.

"Thank you so much for your prayers, I am sure it is that which has kept me on ; I should have broken down long ago, but for that. I must stop now ; I forget we are not sitting over the fire at Wheatley. It was very nice, wasn't it? I hope you are able to keep the same spirit of simplicity and love round about you."

The last letter to this old and valued Wheatley friend has a pathos of its own. It is dated September 8, 1909, exactly six months before he died, when he was in his eightieth year:—

"I am very sorry that I have been so long thanking you for your last letter. I find it very difficult now to do more than attend to important letters of business. I look back to the life at Wheatley with the greatest pleasure; there was a real bond of disinterested love between us all. People now are trying to make themselves happy without religion, but it is a hollow, heartless kind of happiness not worthy of the name. I believe the love of God must stand first, and then, in God, we can love one another. People want to have social security and comfort, but without religion, without the Church. We must hold fast to the old way of the love of God, and the love of one another as taught us in the Bible and the Prayer Book, and we want the Church for the sake of the ministry of the Word and Sacraments, by which God teaches us and gives us His grace. God bless you, dear Charlie, and guide you on to the end, which is really the *great beginning*. Remember me in your prayers, as I do you every day. God bless you, and all like you."

Village life was always a great attraction to him. He loved the simple people and their ways.

"I never could write to you, as if you was a gentleman," wrote a village lad to him in his early days, showing how absolutely a gentleman King was.

Canon Crowfoot, one of his great friends at Lincoln in later life, sets out in the following words how great a help King's early life had been in preparing him for what was to come :—

"He possessed great advantages from the experiences of his home life as a boy. He had lived as a young man in the country, though not in the County of Lincoln. He knew the ground which he was treading ; he knew the life of the cottager ; no squire, or farmer, or groom, or carter knew all the points of a horse better than the bishop. When his knees had gripped the saddle, all the nature of

Wheatley Church.

(*From a photo by H. W. Taunt.*)

Page 32.

the horse had passed into him ; he had performed feats of horsemanship which only the best and boldest of riders are able to achieve. The rod and the gun had been constantly in his hand when he lived as a lad in his father's home ; he knew the hackles and wing-feathers which go to make the most tempting flies for trout and dace and grayling, and he always tied them himself.

"His first and only curacy had been at Wheatley ; but he had learnt there all the ins-and-outs of a cottager's life. No one could describe washing-day, and how the soapsuds fly from the tub, with a Pre-Raphaelite distinctness as the bishop could. He won at once the attention and ever-abiding respect of the good wives who preside over that tub. And so, when some church after restoration was reopened, or some window or pulpit was to be dedicated, and the church was crowded with the neighbouring gentry and farmers from the countryside, as well as with the labourers of the parish itself, the bishop would begin his sermon with some simple incident drawn from their own life—'If I were about to cut a hedge'—and, having caught their attention, he would then lead them on to higher things, and send them away with hearts full of the higher service to which they were called, and of the heavenly home which was being prepared for them."[1]

[1] See *Lincoln Diocesan Magazine*, April, 1910.

CHAPTER III

PRINCIPAL AT CUDDESDON

Diede lor verace fondamento ;
E quel tanto sonò nelle sue guance,
Sì ch' a pugnar, per accender la fede,
Dell' evangelio fero scudo e lance.
Par. xxix. 111–114.

Gave them truth to build on ; and the sound
Was mighty on their lips ; nor needed they,
Beside the Gospel, other spear or shield,
To aid them in their warfare for the Faith.
Cary.

Cuddesdon College.

(*From a photo by Gillman & Co.*)

Page 37.

CHAPTER III

PRINCIPAL AT CUDDESDON

CERTAINLY King loved Wheatley ; often and often in later life his thoughts went back to his early ministerial days spent there ; and he would have been content to stay and work there for the rest of his life. But it was not so ordered.

After four years at Wheatley, in 1858, at the express wish of Bishop Wilberforce, he went as chaplain to Cuddesdon. He was very unwilling to leave Wheatley ; in later life he told an intimate friend that he could remember the exact spot on the road between that village and Cuddesdon where, after talking the matter over with the bishop and after he had rather begged (it would appear) to be allowed to stay on in his parish, Wilberforce at last "kicked his horse and rode off, saying, 'Well, I think you ought to go.'"

There had been troubles and anxieties at Cuddesdon. The college had been founded four years before by Bishop Wilberforce at the beginning of his episcopate. The Rev. Alfred Pott (afterwards Archdeacon of Berkshire) was the first Principal, and he was shortly followed by the Rev. H. H. Swinney. The Rev. Henry Parry Liddon was Vice-Principal, and the Rev. Albert Barff (who later on became head of the choir school, St. Paul's Cathedral)[1] was Chaplain.

Soon after the college had been established it became the object of a controversial attack on its teaching and methods. Considerable excitement was aroused throughout the diocese, and the bishop had felt himself obliged to appoint a commission of inquiry, consisting of the three archdeacons. The report of this commission was on the whole favourable to the work and influence of the college ; but the archdeacons suggested some small modification of existing arrangements in the interests of peace, and in order to reassure any who might be anxious in regard to the tone and teaching of the college.

Bishop Wilberforce never wholly trusted Liddon's methods or point of view, and it was thought that King's influence would have a

[1] He died in 1913, Vicar of St. Giles's, Cripplegate, and Prebendary of St. Paul's.

moderating effect. King therefore became chaplain in place of Barff. Within a year, however, Liddon left Cuddesdon to become Vice-Principal of St. Edmund Hall, Oxford, and the Rev. W. H. Davey[1] took his place at Cuddesdon. In 1863 Swinney died, and Edward King from being chaplain (having stoutly declined to occupy Liddon's place as Vice-Principal in 1859) was made Principal.

These fourteen or fifteen years at Cuddesdon were extraordinarily eventful in regard to King's character and influence. Of a naturally retiring and unassuming disposition, there were those who said of him, "He will never be able to do it." He rose in a wonderful way to the position which he had been called to occupy. He exercised an altogether unique influence over the students; while at the same time, as Vicar of the Parish of Cuddesdon, he won the hearts of the village people.

But the main significance of King's work at Cuddesdon is that he almost entirely revolutionized the methods current in the middle of the last century in regard to the training of the clergy. It is not too much to say that in the 'fifties and 'sixties there was no method in

[1] Afterwards Dean of Llandaff.

the training of the clergy—because there was no training at all for the great majority of ordinands. They went, for the most part, without any special preparation, from "the cricket-fields and the river to the altars of the Church of God."

Certainly there had been a beginning of better things. Colleges at Wells and Chichester had been founded a few years before, and had done excellent work. The name of Pindar, Principal of Wells, will always be had in grateful remembrance; but neither at Wells nor Chichester was there any collegiate life; the students lived in lodgings, and met only for lectures and chapel. It was at Cuddesdon that an altogether fresh beginning was made. The men were gathered there under one roof, and the idea of a common life was developed. The students were all graduates, and went there for a year or two of special training for the work of the ministry. Now it seems the most natural thing in the world. But in 1854, and for a long time afterwards, it was not so. Theological colleges were objects of suspicion; they were too obviously the outcome of the Tractarian Movement. The universities looked askance at them, and exhibited "a one-sided and jealous academical spirit which would make the Faculty of Theology responsible for the education of the clergy." But it is no disparagement to the universities to say that, "apart from some special additional training, they are not entirely suitable places for testing and developing a vocation for the priesthood."

Into what other professions can men enter without some special training? If a man wishes to become efficient in his profession he has to go through the discipline of learning all he can about the work to which he wishes to devote his life. It is, therefore, strange that the ministry could ever have been thought of as the one exception to this rule. You might specialize in all other professions, but somehow or other no special technical knowledge and no special discipline of character was needed for the priesthood. Men were afraid of "narrowing" tendencies. Theological colleges were called "hot-houses," and bishops looked askance at them.

Now what King did more than any one man was, in a very large measure at all events, to show that these prejudices were not really justified. Where so well as in a theological college can a man acquire a knowledge of, and a love for, his sacred profession? A high enthusiasm for the work which lies before him is aroused or stimulated, and he leaves the college after a year or two of special training "determined by God's help to give himself wholly to this one thing," and mentally and morally equipped to begin the work of the ministry.

It is not merely, or chiefly, the intellectual training which has to be thought of, but the moral and spiritual testing and training of character. It is this which is the paramount concern in theological colleges; their work is to deepen and strengthen character, as well as to teach revealed truth. It is to get men "to lay deep and strong in penitence the foundation of their character. It is a place of retirement, where they can fit themselves by discipline and training for the difficult and responsible work of teaching and feeding souls."

It was at Cuddesdon under Edward King that successive generations of men had their character thus deepened and strengthened; they were inspired by high ideals, they learnt to understand and realize the joy of a life really given to God; they found there a veritable home—a home of training and disci-

Dr. King (about 1870).

(From a photo by Hills & Saunders.)

Page 42.

pline, fitting them for their future work. In the unshackled intercourse of such a life they learnt the meaning of brotherly love. They had their wills braced, their affections purified, their intellects quickened, as in the stillness of the little chapel they pondered again and again the great mysteries of the Catholic Faith. There at Cuddesdon they came to apprehend the "gladness and buoyancy" which ought to characterize the Christian life, as in the freedom of social intercourse with friends and teachers "they that feared the LORD spake often one to another."

For King had the extraordinary gift of personal influence which few, if any, could resist. He knew instinctively how to deal with men. His study-door at the vicarage close by was always open, so that the men might go and see him whenever they liked. "There were no rules in my time," he would say in after years; "these came later, and were an improvement." But the truth is there was no need of rules with King—his rule was a rule of love. He used to have very poor health at this time, and was often compelled to rest a good deal when he was not feeling well. When the men saw he was unfit for work they used to devise means of dissuading him from lecturing—"I'm afraid, dear Principal, you will not be able to lecture to-day because all the men have gone into Oxford."

But no words can describe the affection which was felt for him by those who came under his spell. He had an abundance of sanctified common sense and a great gift of "wisdom." Many young men came to Cuddesdon with a good deal of shrinking and misgiving. "They didn't unpack for a fortnight," King would say in later life. One who became well known in after life, the Rev. C. N. Gray,[1] son of the great Bishop of Capetown, came to Cuddesdon not at all pleased with the Principal for not allowing him to bring a horse! He came up, consequently, not in the best possible mood, and somewhat firmly resolved not to do what Mr. King told him. Soon after his arrival on Saturday night he heard a knock at the door of his little room, and the Principal came in. "O, Mr. Gray," he said—"I came to tell you that there is service in the church at eight o'clock to-morrow morning; but, very likely, you will be tired with your journey—so mind you don't get up

[1] Vicar of Helmsley.

till after breakfast ; it is better not to do so if you are tired."

Mr. Gray was a young man of iron constitution, and resented the idea of being tired ; so he immediately expressed his intention of being in church at eight next morning. In a very short time "Charlie Gray" and the Principal became fast friends and remained so all through their lives.

The life and work of Cuddesdon is well described in the following letter from one who was a student there in Dr. King's time :—[1]

"Cuddesdon life was felt to be the most delightful life which we had ever experienced. Our numbers were not too large for a sense of family affection and closeness of intercourse. There was a tinge of cloistered retirement, of common spiritual interest, which made it possible, without any sense of presumption or sacrilege, to speak of the longings and aspirations closest to our hearts, and for those to whom spiritual life was a comparatively new thing to be aided by the longer experience of more proficient friends. Example also was most

[1] Rev. J. E. Swallow, Chaplain to the House of Mercy, Horbury.

effective. It was impossible to see the effect of careful thanksgiving after Communion, and of regular meditation in chapel, upon the lives, and even the faces, of the devout students, and not be drawn to strive after some share in it.

"But above all these was the influence and the life and instruction of Dr. King. We had never known such sermons, such meditations: it was a new experience to find a good man full of such affectionate interest in our individual spiritual welfare. His lectures on systematic Christian doctrine were a veritable *théologie affective*, in which the dry bones of dogma were clothed with the sensitive flesh of living, loving devotion, and lit up with the glow of poetic contemplation, often under the guidance of Dante. We were first awed by the consideration of the responsibilities of the preacher, and later inspired with the longing to put in practice the directions which made it seem possible for us to speak for God to souls.

"The student-preacher of a written sermon, twice a week, after Evensong before the college, had the right to dine at the vicarage and receive a detailed criticism after dinner. The extempore preacher, once a week, had a short stroll in the garden, or an interview

The Library, Cuddesdon College.

Page 46.

in the study after Matins. Practical hints on the Visitation of the Sick were enlivened by details of personal experience ; and we learnt the possibility of training a devout chronic sufferer to appreciate the ancient offices of the Church. Hooker was illustrated by references to questions of the day, Butler by the application of his principles to what had just happened in the village or the college. The dominant note of all was intelligent sympathy. There was a genuine ring in the 'Dear People' from the pulpit. . . . We felt it most for ourselves ; we were most tenderly, yet most unflinchingly, compelled to face our lives before God. Until now we had never understood ourselves. At last the tangle was unravelled by one as familiar, it seemed, with its every twist and turn as if he had himself lived it out along with us. Doctrine, sermon, meditation — each went home with direct personal application until it was plain that our only course was to submit our lives and difficulties, our temptations and sins, our hopes and fears, to one who seemed to know them all without needing to be told, and so benefit by the guidance for the future of one who had shown himself clairvoyant of the past. *Qui non ardet, non incendit*—we struck out the negatives as we looked up to him; we found them for ourselves. *Mundamini, qui fertis vasa Domini*—we dared not stretch out our hands for consecration, uncleansed with the purification of the sanctuary. The result was that men felt they owed their souls to him."

Cuddesdon brought out all King's gaiety and playfulness. He was absolutely at home with the young men, and they with him. He loved the work and the life, and used to look back upon it with the utmost gratitude and affection.

In January, 1908, the bishop wrote to an old student:—

"Thank you so much for your loving words: 'He loved them to the end'! This is our standard. I was seventy-eight two Sundays ago! So you must keep up your love a little longer, and then in Paradise it will (D.V.) be like Cuddesdon again."

"He had a strong sense of humour," writes Canon Brooke, "which he often employed with very good effect. Many a rebuke (where such was needed) or a piece of unwelcome advice, was given in a way that could not possibly cause pain to the most sensitive nature.

"One Good Friday, I remember, it was reported to the principal that a certain student had taken hardly any nourishment during the previous week. In a few minutes the aforesaid student received the following note: 'Dearest man, eat breakfast, and come down to the lower level of yours, E.K.'

"At another time a student, who was a great sportsman, announced to the Principal his intention of going out to Africa as a missionary, and the answer was—'Wouldn't you like it! You are to go and work in the slums of Bristol.'" [1]

Another old student [2] writes:—

"The admiration which the Principal used to express for the spiritual guides of an earlier generation was a lesson to us in 'hero-worship.' Canon Carter, of Clewer, and Mr. Milman of Marlow (afterwards Bishop of Calcutta), were among our devotional lecturers at Ember seasons, for as yet in the sixties

[1] The *Treasury*, for April, 1910.

[2] Rev. D. Elsdale, Rector of Little Gransden, who was a student at Cuddesdon in 1861, and chaplain from 1861 till 1866.

H

Retreats for ordinands were scarcely organized. Another of our spiritual instructors was Father Benson, who was already living a community life in Iffley Road with Father Grafton and Father O'Neill. Of Father Benson, King used to say that it was only his sense of humour which kept him alive! Many of his sayings abide in one's memory, as when on one occasion, after the country labourer had been given the franchise, King said, 'We must now learn to work *with* our people rather than *for* them.' To me the Parochialia Lectures were the most fruitful of all his utterances, whereas Canon Keymer[1] tells me that *he* cherishes, above all other influences, the addresses in chapel; and he recalls an address on *The Priesthood*, after which he said, 'Please lend me your notes;' whereupon the Principal smiled, and handed to him a scrap of paper on which was inscribed the one word, 'Ἱέρευς.'

"Canon Keymer adds that one of the most instructive of his actions was the tenderness with which he used to conduct his mother to Church for the daily evensong.

[1] Rev. Nathaniel Keymer, Rector of Headon, 1879–1917; Proctor in Convocation for the Diocese of Southwell, 1904–1916.

"All who were present on the occasion of the memorable farewell to Cuddesdon in the Palace Gardens on Trinity Tuesday, 1873, will remember the presentation by Vice-Principal Willis of the Principal's portrait to Mrs. King as part of the Cuddesdon farewell gift. It seemed to many of us who were there a most touching comment on his constant teaching of the claims of filial love and devotion when King, after thanking the subscribers on his mother's behalf, left them for a time to go straight home with her as she was beginning to get very tired.

"I applied to a former office-bearer of the college to give me some impressions of his influence, and he sagaciously wrote these three causes :—

"'He was himself an absolutely saintly character.

"'He was, and always acted as, an English gentleman.

"'He sought to be, and generally succeeded in being, fair in judgement.'

"If I may venture to add one feature to this threefold estimate I will specify the reality of his love for *all* with whom he was brought into regular or casual contact, in spite of incongruities which, we could see, jarred on his sensitive nature, while the ardency of his affections was poured out upon some to whom he was drawn by a divine instinct. This theological virtue of love reminds me of a note in his precious Parochialia Lectures :—

"'The requirements of a good sermon are—Church doctrine, Catholic phraseology, Study of Scripture, and the whole tied together by Love.'

"The deliberate and the unconscious influence of such a person in such a college had manifold results mostly unknown to us till the great day of account. Yet we have known men converted by the HOLY SPIRIT of GOD working through him ; we have known his influence lead to the sanctification of many beautiful characters, and we know that it was the revelation to hundreds of us of the incomparable glory of the ministerial life."

This period of King's life was coincident with a development of his own Church standpoint. He had been brought up in good Church principles, as these were commonly understood sixty or seventy years ago ; but from Charles Marriott and others in Oxford his convictions became more and more clearly defined, and at Cuddesdon they developed still more.

In the matter of Confession, for example. Liddon had made a great point of it with the students, but when King became principal he had not himself been to Confession; and on one of the men asking him to hear his confession, his reply was, "Wait a little, I must make my own first." And he soon afterwards rode into Oxford and made his first confession to Dr. Pusey. Long years afterwards he told a friend that the doctor (as he called Pusey) had given him the 103rd Psalm for a penance.

Somewhat later, especially at Oxford, he was greatly sought after as a confessor and spiritual adviser. A very large number of undergraduates must have made their first confessions to him between 1873 and 1885.

As a spiritual guide he was extraordinarily gentle and hopeful. His way was always to encourage people as much as possible. He would often say, "You must not let temptation take the heart out of you. You must go bravely and quietly on." After absolution had been given he would always offer up extemporary prayer with wonderful insight and directness of application to the wants of the particular penitent, and then he would give his blessing, ending up with the words of St. Paul in the Epistle to the Romans, praying that God would guide you and strengthen you and uphold you and "give you all joy and peace in believing, that you may abound in hope through the power of the Holy Ghost."

He himself used Confession up to the last; he did not go often, but it was his habit to go at all events two or three times in the year; and his feeling about this matter in later life was, that it would not be amiss if some of the people who use Confession very frequently would go less often; while he wished that many who never go to Confession would do so now and then. His words to one who had known him for many years were: "Don't you think, dear friend, that it would be a good thing if some people did not go *quite* so often as they do, and if some who do not go at all would go sometimes?"

It was at Cuddesdon that King had a very strong presentiment that he would not live to be older than forty-two, and it so happened that on his forty-second birthday he was called to visit a man stricken down with small-pox, a disease of which there had been some other

Dr. King (Presentation portrait on leaving Cuddesdon).

(From an engraving by T. L. Atkinson of a portrait by George Richmond, R.A., 1873.)

Page 55.

cases in the village. The man eventually died, and so great was the fear of infection that no one could be found to put him in his coffin. King went, made the necessary arrangements, placed the body in the coffin, and, as he said, "screwed him down," and then went back to the vicarage, feeling sure that his presentiment would come true. Mercifully it was not so; he did not, in fact, catch the disease at all. In after years he was heard sometimes to speak of this occurrence, and to use it as a warning to the young not to be led away, or hampered, or terrified by such presentiments, which are often altogether misleading.

So the fourteen years of his life passed swiftly and happily away in work which was thoroughly congenial to King. As vicar of the parish he was kept in touch with the simple and poor people whom he loved with all his heart and soul; while as Principal of the college he was, as we have seen, consciously or otherwise, transforming current ideas as to the training of the clergy. He went abroad, and visited the more important seminaries in France, and picked up what hints he could. He was English and an English Churchman to the core, so there was never the least danger of his trying to turn Englishmen into foreigners or implanting French ideas on to English minds. What he did was to grasp the fundamental fact that to bring men to Christ you must yourself be living as close to Him as possible; and, therefore, that the training of the clergy meant primarily, as we have seen, the sanctification of the character; and he bent all his efforts towards making a Christ-like clergy. With this end in view he was, as he might have said, audacious in his exercise of personal influence.

The students were taught to aim at sanctifying themselves for the sake of those to whom they hoped one day to minister. They felt that the father of the family at Cuddesdon bore them in his heart, and was giving his best in order to help them to get further away from sin and nearer to God; that he was entirely himself in all this, incapable of pose or unreality or artificiality of any sort; but a man endued with singular gifts of the Holy Ghost—extraordinarily attractive and sympathetic and winning; extraordinarily gentle, and yet amazingly strong and brave.

Six years after he had left the college, King

had an opportunity of telling the world what he thought about Cuddesdon and his life there.

A pamphlet had been published in 1879 by the Rev. C. J. Elliott, attacking a book called *The Communicant's Manual*, to which King had written a preface.

The point of Mr. Elliott's charge was that the book was written for the use of the students at Cuddesdon ; and that it was calculated to teach them false opinions about the Real Presence, the Eucharistic Sacrifice, and Confession. In replying, King, while rebutting the charge of heterodoxy, wrote the following beautiful *apologia* for Cuddesdon :—

"The book which you have made the medium of your attack was never written for Cuddesdon, nor in any sense enjoined for the use of the students ; nor can I remember recommending it for their use ; but I am grateful for this opportunity of publicly uniting myself once more with a place in which I spent fourteen of the happiest years of my life, receiving kindnesses and blessings which I can never repay ; and yet, after all, it was not the place, but the teaching and the life, which made Cuddesdon so dear to us. There we lived in the daily enjoyment of the friendship of English hearts, strengthened, softened, perfected by the full power of the whole Catholic Faith.

"There is no need for me to speak of the Cuddesdon students past or present (in spirit they are all one)—they would not wish it; but, for the sake of the poor, to whom they devote their fortunes and their lives, I cannot keep silence.

"Their lives have been to me, and to many others, an evidence of the truth of Christianity, and of the living power of the English Church—in other words, Cuddesdon has been, and is, one of our best defences against infidelity and Rome. Her students have not sought money or patronage from the world; one thing have they desired—liberty to tell the poor 'the whole counsel of God!'"

Perhaps nothing expresses better what Cuddesdon meant to King than some words he spoke to the old Cuddesdon students who gathered round him some years later in the chapter house of St. Paul's, just after his consecration as Bishop of Lincoln:—

"At Cuddesdon, you know, we never thought of being bishops—we didn't care for rank or position.

"Two things we did care for—

"The possession of the whole counsel of God, and liberty to teach it in every way. We wished to offer up our life and be happy, blessed in ourselves, and with the privilege of giving that blessedness to others.

"This was what made Cuddesdon to be Cuddesdon, and drew us nearer to God and to one another ; giving us the peculiar freedom and elasticity which made us so loose and free (though not wild) in head and heart. For our heads rested, bowed down before the full Catholic Faith ; and our hearts were surrendered to be disentangled and disciplined, to find their rest when given up to God. ('For our heart is restless till it finds its rest in Thee.') We were brought to love God, and one another in God, in a real and special way, not understood by people unless they themselves knew what it is to be thus free. . . . All grows really clear by taking God for our rest and end, with a sense of the reality of love and need of discipline. It gives a wonderful power of expansion as the love of God and man is proved as a rule of life."

1. Rev. Geo. Wharton (Radley).
2.
3. Rev. Canon Barnett (a Chaplain).
4. Rev. Geo. Hooper.
5. Bishop Kilner (Richmond).
6. Rev. Piers Claughton.
7. Rev. George Kemp.
8. Rev. Dr. Warburton (Iffley).
9. Archdeacon E. Moore.
10.
11. Rev. C. O. Miles (Banbury).
12. J. Carter, Esq. (father of the Rev. V. Carter).
13.
14. Archdeacon C. Mackarness.
15. Michael Furse (now Bishop of Pretoria.)
16. Rev. A. R. Cartwright (St. John's, Clevedon).
17. Rev. Vernon Carter (Abingdon).
18. Bishop Balfour (Assistant, Bloemfontein).
19.
20. Canon Noel Freeling.
21. Bishop Copleston (of Calcutta).
22. Mrs. Carter.
23. Rev. A. Hutton (St. Barnabas, Oxford.)
24. Rev. the Hon. Albert Lyttelton.
25. Rev. Canon Sturges (Wokingham).
26. Rev. Arthur Lethbridge (Shepton Beauchamp).
27. Rev. Henry Morgan.
28. Rev. G. H. Swinney (Missionary in Africa).
29. Rev. O. J. Reichel.
30. Rev. E. R. Dowdeswell.
31.
32. Rev. the Hon. R. Parsons.
33. Rev. F. J. Kiddle.
34.
35.
36.
37. Rev. Canon Maul.
38. Rev. H. S. Iredell (Tunbridge Wells).
39. Rev. R. J. Wilson (Keble).
40. Rev. E. Ibbotson (then Curate, Dorchester).
41. Rev. J. C. Field.
42.
43. Rev. G. Sankey.
44. Rev. F. A. G. Eichbaum.
45.
46. Mrs. Mackarness.
47. Hon. Lady Coleridge.
48. Mrs. Furse.
49. Mrs. Warburton.
50. Bishop King.
51. Bishop Forbes.
52. Bishop Mackarness.
53. Rev. Aubrey Moore.
54. Bishop Webb.
55. Canon Furse.
56. Henry Barnett, Esq.
57. Archdeacon Pott.
58. Canon Liddon.
59. Rev. E. F. Willis (Calcutta Mission).
60. Mrs. Inge.
61. Hon. Mrs. Randal Parsons.
62.
63. Miss Mackarness.
64. Mrs. Abraham.
65. Archdeacon of Oxford.
66.
67. Archdeacon Cecil Bourke.
68. Rev. Canon Porter (First Student).
69. Miss Bessie Furse (Mrs. Maud).
70. Rev. Ernest Bridgeman.
71. Rev. M. Kelly (Kelly House, Devon).
72.
73.
74. Mrs. W. F. Norris (Deanery, York).
75.
76. Mrs. Cotton.

Cuddesdon Festival, 1875.

From Photograph by H. W. Taunt, Oxford.

CHAPTER IV

PASTORAL PROFESSOR AT OXFORD

Amore,
Acceso di virtù, sempre altro accese,
Pur che la fiamma sua paresse fuore.

Purg. xxii. 10–12.

Let its pure flame
From virtue flow, and love can never fail
To warm another's bosom, so the light
Shine manifestly forth.

Cary.

CHAPTER IV

PASTORAL PROFESSOR AT OXFORD

THE Chair of Pastoral Theology, carrying with it a Canonry at Christ Church, had been founded in 1842.

The first occupant of this important post was the Rev. C. A. Ogilvie. He died in February, 1873. A few days later Mr. Gladstone, with the sanction of the Queen, wrote to Dr. King, asking him to assume the vacant chair. "Allow me to assure you," he writes, "that in submitting your name to Her Majesty I have been moved by no other consideration than that of what I believe to be your gifts and merits, and the promise they afford of a tranquil but powerful and deep religious influence on young men within the precincts of the university." How abundantly this hope was fulfilled the young men who happened to be at Oxford for the next twelve years could abundantly testify. But for the moment the loss to Cuddesdon was terrible.

King, though installed at Christ Church in April, did not, however, actually vacate the principalship till after the annual festival, which was held, as usual, on the Tuesday after Trinity Sunday, which fell in 1873 on June 10th. It was naturally a great occasion. Liddon was the preacher, and in the sermon he alluded, of course, to what was uppermost in the minds of all. "To-day . . . is a day of many congratulations, natural and legitimate. Never before the present year has this college, in the person of any of its working officers, received such emphatic recognition from high quarters of the services which it has been permitted to render to the Church. That recognition many of you will feel, however grateful in itself, is purchased at a very heavy cost." [1]

King settled in Christ Church with his mother for the October Term. He used laughingly to tell how kind the undergraduates were to him on his beginning his new work. All sorts of rumours about his ritualistic leanings had gained currency in Oxford and not least at Christ Church, but "all the dear

[1] The sermon is printed in *Clerical Life and Work* under the title "The Moral Groundwork of Clerical Training."

Tom Quad, Christ Church, Oxford.

(Dr. King's lodgings are to be seen on the left hand. From a photo by H. W. Taunt.)

Page 65.

things (i.e. the undergraduates) did," he used to say, "was to hang up a surplice on the lamp-post outside my house." It was a not unkindly welcome, as much as to say, "We know what to expect!"

At that time Christ Church was a very strong centre of Church influence. Dr. Pusey was still alive in the well-known corner of Tom Quad; Liddon was close by on the other side of the great gateway. Dr. Bright, as Professor of Ecclesiastical History, was in his house opposite "Kill Canon" archway, a hundred yards from King's "Lodgings"; and among younger men Henry Scott Holland and Francis Paget were soon to come to the front as Senior Students of the House.

This was an atmosphere in which King could breathe freely. He was not naturally "academic" in any way, less still was there ever any trace of "donnishness" in him, so that at first sight his professorship might have seemed a formidable task to take up; but with those who have been named in such close proximity he would not feel stifled or strained; on the contrary, he would be thoroughly at home, in complete sympathy, and in an atmosphere in which he would naturally and inevitably expand.

Not that he in any way neglected the intellectual side of things. Far from it. Many who knew him as only a good and holy man, and who may have somewhat deprecated his coming to Oxford as a professor, soon learnt to realize that they had in King one who was richly endowed with the gift of wisdom, and one whose opinion in intellectual questions was very well worth having. Men soon came to discover his great ability.

He used to lecture each year on Hooker, on the Ordinal, and on Pastoral Theology. His lectures were given in his own house. The men crowded into his study and the dining-room adjoining, and King, wearing his cassock, but no gown, used to stand in the doorway between the two apartments. It was more like talking than lecturing, but none the less—probably the more—appreciated for all that. He was naturally best, because most at home, in his lectures on Pastoral Theology. His experience at Wheatley and Cuddesdon was, of course, invaluable. His lectures on preaching many will remember.

He used to say about the test of a good sermon—"That sermon is a good sermon not when people come out of church saying,

'What a wonderful sermon, what a wonderful preacher,' but when they go quietly away and want to be alone."

"Any manner but no mannerism," was another of his sayings about sermons. You can use any manner, he would say, that is natural to *you*, but don't copy somebody else's manner. Be natural, be yourself, and any action you may use will then be spontaneous and inevitable. "Truth conveyed through a personality," is one great definition of preaching.[1] He used to dwell also on Bishop Dupanloup's description of preaching. It is speaking *to* the people (*parler à*), not merely speaking *before* them (*devant*). "You may fire off a great sermon before people," he would say, "but it won't touch them unless you speak to them." He had himself the power of a real orator, but *ars est artium celare artem*—and his preaching seemed the simplest thing in the world. When he wrote or spoke he talked *to* the people, using often the simplest words and illustrations. He used to say that it was good to begin with an allusion to something that was in people's minds, and this was his own constant practice. He was never

[1] The phrase is Bishop Phillips Brooks'.

inappropriate ; he would warn men against repeating a "Sunday evening gaslight sermon," which had done very well in a big town, to a small country congregation in a village.

Again and again he would insist on St. Augustine's three words as to the purpose of a sermon—*Doceat*, *delectet*, *moveat*—it must teach, interest, and persuade ; it must address the whole man.

A sermon should be like a church. There is the porch or introduction, which should be short ; say what you are going to preach about. Then there is the nave, the main theme of the sermon divided into two or three bays. Finally there is the chancel, which represents the conclusion. Get the three main parts into right proportions.

In later life, though his sermons were often written on bits of paper of all sizes and shapes, he would say that an envelope opened out and bent backwards made a very good ground for a sermon. The central part of the envelope was for the main theme, the two sides, when it was split open, served as space for jotting down the illustrations, the top and bottom ends for the beginning and the conclusion respectively.

He preached constantly in Oxford, especially

"Bethel."

Page 68.

at St. Barnabas and at St. Philip and St. James. But perhaps his greatest work in Oxford—his most far-reaching work—was done in the altogether informal "Friday Addresses," which he gave at nine o'clock every week in an out-house which was reached by passing through the professor's house and across the lawn. This building was converted by King into an oratory, which was eventually somewhat enlarged, and which must have held about one hundred and fifty men. This was his "Bethel," as he called it, and every Friday in term time it was crowded by young men. No ritual here—all was absolute simplicity. "It was a wash-house," he said, "and we cleaned it out, and put in cocoa-nut matting and chairs and a harmonium—very simple, but very lovely. It is a great pleasure to me." The walls were quite bare, with the exception of Guido Reni's "Head of Christ," which hung above a fald-stool at the end of the building.

The place was full before the time to begin, and when "Tom" struck nine—one can feel again, after so many years—the hush of expectation, then the opening of the door, followed by the heavy tread, and, finally, the sight of the well-known figure, as King, robed in a very ample and somewhat crumpled surplice, made his way up the room and knelt down at the faldstool ; there was a pause, then a collect, followed by a hymn (sung kneeling), accompanied by a harmonium ; then a prayer, after which he would stand up and speak as he alone could speak. It might be on the Lord's Prayer, or on the Ten Commandments, or on the seven capital sins, or on our Lord's life ; but, whatever the subject, it was so handled as to seem to go straight to men's hearts. Current events would be alluded to—the beginning of term, the weather, the death of General Gordon, an article in the *Times*—these and suchlike topics would be touched on ; but it seemed to matter little what the subject was. What we all felt was that here was a heart beating in sympathy with my heart ; it would help me if I could talk to him ; and he wants me to live close to God so that I may bring others to God ; for that was always his point of view. He knew that many—probably the majority—of those to whom he spoke would be looking forward to Ordination, and he would often say, "I am speaking, dear friends, to you like this for the sake of the poor people to whom you will, please God, be going."

"Of course," writes Mr. George Russell,[1] "his official duties were primarily concerned with the candidates for Holy Orders; but his influence extended to a much wider circle. Men who, with no thought of seeking the priesthood, were yet in earnest about religion, found themselves drawn by an irresistible attraction to the private lectures which he gave at his house at Christ Church. Those lectures dealt, not with disputed points of doctrine, but with the deepest and often the most secret facts of moral and spiritual experience. His power of sympathy amounted to genius, and gave him an almost supernatural insight into human hearts. He combined the keenest spirituality with a sanctified common sense, which good people sometimes lack. He spoke to us of our past lives, of our future prospects, of our present temptations, of our besetting sins, with an intimate penetration, engendered by long experience in personal contact with souls. He told us truths about ourselves which were part of our consciousness, but which we believed to have been hidden from all except ourselves. It was the same when he preached before the university. There was no rhetoric, no striving

[1] *Edward King*, p. 55.

after effect, no parade of learning, no attempt to be startling or novel or paradoxical. . . . There was the clear statement of theological truth, so gently worded that even the most fiercely controverted questions were touched without offence or jar. There were plain lessons of moral duty, from which one might shrink, but which one could not gainsay. And every now and then there was some keen phrase about our experience, past or present, which once heard was never forgotten : 'Some of us look back to-night to old school friendships when Satan was transformed into an angel of light.'"

No picture of Dr. King at Oxford would be complete without some reference to his mother.

The Bishop of Winchester writes : "The only thing that made the uniqueness of King feel less unique was to know Mrs. King. But to see how the nature had come to him, upon which the special work of grace and discipline had wrought, only made it the more attractive. His ways with her were delightful :—

"'My dear mother, you know, always tells people, with so much content, that she pays

Mrs. King.

age 72.

her servants just the same wages as many years ago. She does not know how they come into my study from the drawing-room on wages-day and receive a nice little addition.'

"Her death made a great difference in his life. I remember one quaint instance of it. A preacher had preached in the cathedral a sermon which he thoroughly disliked: taste and temper, form and substance. He remarked afterwards, 'Now a sermon like that makes me feel how I miss my dear mother. I should have just gone into her room afterwards and said, "Mother, we've had a *beastly* sermon!" and then there would have been an end of it, i.e. all the rankle of it would have gone.' His father, when dying, had commended his mother to his special charge; and she was at Cuddesdon and Oxford, till her death, the recipient of all his confidences and the centre of his life."

"So your dear, sweet mother is gone to her rest," wrote Dr. Jones, the Bishop of Capetown, "and to the bosom of Jesus Christ. May the light of God's face shine ever more and more upon her! She was indeed one of this earth's treasures, a jewel of God's storehouse. What a change this will make in your life!

. . . I had learnt quite to love her, and I had learnt to regard her as my ideal of the Christian lady."

"Through all the Cuddesdon, and most of the Oxford, time, the most delightfully characteristic feature of his home was his mother. She had his gracious, tender ways, and it was an infinite joy to play round her with his fun. One of the prettiest sights in the world was to watch him open the little side-door into their garden out of the cathedral, and pass through with her, after service. We used to wonder how he would ever bear her departure. But when her death came we found that he had been preparing himself for years, and that he could retain all his wonderful serenity and gentleness and confidence and courage.

"'My great satisfaction,' he wrote 'is that the victory was so complete. I did not expect any fear; but there was not one word of anxiety or care about anything—just the same trustful, bright, loving self she has always been. . . . How to get on I do not quite see, but then I need not move just yet; I am sure the light will come. I have had so many kind letters speaking of her brightness, sympathy, wisdom, etc. And, when I remember that she has been enabled to do all this in the days of her widowhood, it is a bright example for me, and gives me hope. Pray for me, dear friend, a little bit that I may be guided. I am tempted to fear the loss of her wisdom almost more than the comfort of her brightness ; but I know whence it came, and it can come still.' "[1]

A leading characteristic of Edward King was what one who knew him very intimately calls his "ethical outlook." All his reading was done with this idea in view. His books continually bear witness to it. He marked any passage or phrase which bore on the development or enrichment of character. Thus he developed continually his natural insight into character by what he read.

When he first went back to Oxford he re-read his Aristotle and took the *Ethics* as a basis ; and used them, not indeed as an end, but as a beginning. "To go from the Bible to Aristotle," he says, " is to go *back* and to go *down*, and to narrow your hold on, and your sympathy with, men. The old taunt, 'Oh ! can't you write a better ethic ? Why, as

[1] Canon H. Scott Holland, in *A Bundle of Memories*.

Christians do you keep going back to Aristotle?' is answered—'We *do* see the deficiencies in Aristotle, we are *not* satisfied with him. We *can* and we *do* supply the deficiencies in *revelation*.'"

He longed for some one to bring out a good book on Christian Ethics.

"Political Economy," he writes to Henry Scott Holland, à propos of the labour troubles and strikes which were taking place in the year 1877, "the relation of ethics and politics, is becoming a practical question, and I very much hope some of you good people will bring out an edition of the *Republic* adapted for a *Christian Ploughboy*, with notes in *his* language, and illustrated not by arguments but by *stories*. We have been worrying these poor boys with the Proverbs, and little narrow bits of personal ethics, and now they are beginning to feel there is a big world round about them, with lots of new powers and hopes, and so they are dashing about. But we must put them upon the real principle, and then, after a bit, they will go on and up, in order, dear things!"

Another letter shows to some extent how he would apply his principles.

"I hope the farmer's lad will do well. The best way is to point out certain plain fundamental things for him to know and do. Get the main outline of his life right, and trust to the Holy Spirit to aid him in all those delicate and divine intricacies of the spiritual life which our clumsy faculties are for the most part too rough to touch without injury. I mean teach him the Ten Commandments, Creed, and Lord's Prayer; to act from a sense of right and wrong, instead of pleasure. Teach him to pray for himself, to keep from persons and places where he would be likely to go wrong; to read the Bible, if he can; and keep Sunday quietly, and go to church. That plain kind of way is best. Your own loving heart will probably be the best power to draw him, but you must take care to draw him by your heart, to God, and not simply to yourself. It is heartbreaking work, but God will help you, if you first give yourself to Him. God bless you and keep you and guide you with His wisdom and holy love." All this keen and intense love for individual souls was never merely emotional or sentimental or weak; it was part and parcel of his intellectual outlook on the world and on human society and human life.

"Intellectually he has sometimes been depreciated, perhaps because he won no academic distinctions. But those who knew him will perhaps think that he was among the most intellectual persons they have ever known; only, as was perhaps the case with St. Anselm, to whom he has been compared, his intelligence was so much a part of his character, so wholly himself, that it might easily escape notice in the simplicity and charm of his personality. He had a singularly alert mind, and was interested in everything; no one ever saw him bored, and he never touched a topic without displaying an original view, and he was really alive to the intellectual difficulties of his day. He knew and could talk French, German, and Italian; and in a mixed company he could talk in at least three languages at once—no small accomplishment; while his English was admirable, and he read widely to the end."[1]

In 1875 King spent some of the Long Vacation in Dresden. He lived in a German family, and his remarks on German methods illustrate his wisdom and discernment. They

[1] Dr. F. E. Brightman in *Dictionary of English Church History*, p. 308.

are certainly not without special interest at this moment.

"I had," he writes, "a very interesting week at Leipzig, and saw most of the chief theological professors—Delitzsch, Ludthard, and Tholuck—at Halle, about twenty miles off. They are very simple, and work very hard at their books; but not very much more, I think. I think in England we have a wider-reaching and better balanced work than the Germans have; they have confined themselves almost to the cultivation of the intellect, and I don't think it will hold the *whole* man; he needs cultivation of heart, feelings, affections, etc., as well."

And again, after his return home, he writes: "I have been in Dresden this Long Vacation, working at German. It is very interesting seeing the wonderful upgrowth and power of the German nation; but the unbelief is very sad—only three per cent., they say, go to any sort of church in Berlin, and unbelief is quite open. They seem to have passed through the stages of Rationalism and Pantheism, and now they have almost ceased to care about the metaphysics which we have been following, and *worshipping* in them, and they are devoting themselves to physics. This means, I fear, for many, *materialism*. Ludthard says this plainly, meaning by materialism love of money or power or pleasure ; this seems to be the leading danger now—that people will try to be respectable, but without God ; to separate morality from religion, to devote themselves to civilization and culture, and forget God. The results of physical science are so directly beneficial to society that it pays in the eyes of the world ; and yet one ought to know by this time, after the example of Greece and Rome, that culture may exist without morality."

There is something almost prophetic in these words.

In a letter to the present writer the Bishop of Winchester [1] says : "I owe immensely much to that beloved and holy man." It was a great event to us who already had knowledge of him when the news came that Mr. Gladstone was sending King to us as Professor of Pastoral Theology. We knew that he would do the work in some ways most admirably, for to all Cuddesdon men, and to

[1] Dr. Talbot.

many others by repute, the Principal's Pastoralia were something by themselves. But we hardly knew how he would fit in to the academical surroundings. He had been so identified with his quiet and beautiful surroundings at Cuddesdon that, joyful as we were to welcome him, we wondered how it would go.

"He himself with his quick, delicate tact and perception, felt acutely how great a change it was; and what a venture of faith for a man without academical distinction and experience; how difficult and even formidable a place a university is to enter in advanced middle life; how he would be in contact with new problems, or old problems in a new atmosphere. I remember his telling me once that when he came to Oxford he took for his special theme of meditation and symbolic remembrance the Crown of Thorns—the Saviour's sufferings of the head—and he intimated that in his inner experience he had found at first the truth of the symbolism. It was very characteristic, solemn, grave, and deep, yet with just that lightest touch of the quaint gracefulness which so often showed itself in lighter ways, and made his conversation and company so delicious. He always keenly felt the difference between himself and academical folk, and the want of familiarity with academical studies and ways of thought. He would express this in his own whimsical way by speaking to us dons as 'You great people'; shall I say that this was three parts modesty and sincerity, and one part irony—so good for us too, and absolutely without sting.

"I never remember, however, any but one time when he seemed a little out of his element; and that was when one could feel that from a sense of duty he had put a strong constraint upon his natural instincts. He was preaching in the university pulpit; there had been some controversy about Confession. It was a subject on which he could have spoken out of a full experience with a characteristic blending of sympathy and firmness; but he evidently thought it his duty to preach a learned sermon; and to his modesty it seemed best to do this by appeal to great names and Fathers of the Church rather than say much of his own, so he gave us quite a chain of patristic and other quotations; and it was 'dull,' not least perhaps to those to whom the word dull was the last epithet which they would ever have thought themselves likely to use of any utterance from that tender, humorous, pungent, winning spirit.

"By way of contrast I always remember a sermon which he preached as Vicar of Cuddesdon to his parish folk. It was autumn after the harvest was over; and he suggested how the darker evenings might be used for more study of the Old Testament, and for preaching about it in course. The parson ought not to be always exhorting his people, but expounding, and guiding their thoughts; only they hindered this by the need of so much stirring and reminding: 'You make us so noisy in our preaching.' But there was so much to explore in the Books of the Old Testament, if we could give time to books mostly so little known — *Now Nahum!*

"But coming back to his position in the university, it did, I think, prove more intensive than extensive. He did not become a great personality in the university. The dons, on the whole, hardly found out his charm, insight, and cleverness.

"His weapons were not quite academical ones. But the old characteristic influence came out in Oxford, intensive and personal still, but now upon a broader field and with larger reach. It found two special channels.

"There was that of the chair. His professorial lectures (I never heard them)—but perhaps they were not altogether such as the word 'professorial' would naturally suggest. But they were worked for carefully. I remember how he talked of the big work on Pastoral Theology, by Sailer, Bishop of Ratisbon, at which he had worked hard, and his was a pastoral chair; and in that line of teaching he was inimitable, so human, so sagacious, so penetrating, so devout. The spell was felt at once. His class rolled up to unprecedented figures, and hundreds of the young candidates for Holy Orders went out from Oxford carrying with them not only such and such convictions which he had helped to form in his interpretation of Hooker, but even more with thoughts and hints about dealing with their flocks of which they must have felt the touch most in the least controversial and most practical parts of their work. It was the old influence of the Cuddesdon Parochialia deepened and widened.

"The other influence was 'Bethel,' the little outhouse at the end of his garden which he transformed into a little shrine of teaching and devotion. Here on the Friday evenings came numbers of men to join in a simple service and hear him pour out freely the fruits of his sympathy and experience, his insight into divine things and into human life, specially young life.

"But I must not leave the impression that his influence was limited to undergraduates. It was nowhere stronger than in what it brought to some of us younger dons; of this it is a little difficult to speak. Perhaps I can speak of it best by speaking abstractly of his place in the current of the theological movement. No one indeed was less abstract, or more concrete himself than Dr. King. And the knowledge that he was there among us; the living evidence given by his spirit and example of what goodness could be in one who was within our own immediate ken and touch—this was to myself, and I am sure to others of us, a debt for which to be immeasurably thankful.

"But where did he come into the process of Church life in Oxford? Two things stand out.

"He was an affectionate follower of the Tractarians, a son of the great leaders, the contemporary and close friend of the second generation, such as Dr. Liddon and Dr. Bright, and a profound admirer of Dean Church, with whom I have always felt that he had a certain likeness in temperament on some sides. His theology was their theology. He was *si quis alius*, a revering disciple. Yet we all felt at once a new quality in his outlook and treatment of this. He was less severe, less didactic and dominating, less preoccupied than they. With a delightful tact he would just let us hear athwart his modesty (he would never have dreamt of being classed in comparison with them) a note of conscious, even deliberate, difference. His temperament radiated sympathy, mental as well as moral and personal. He felt with men, he felt with his time, he was conscious of the movement under his feet. It did not carry him away, but there was appeal in it; he felt the appeal, and responded to it. He wanted to learn as well as to guide; and I feel sure, looking back, that as he got an increasing position he felt drawn to give younger men the sympathy and help which can be given by one who, standing between generations, can feel something of the new as well as the old.

"I think this can be, perhaps, best illustrated by that portrait of his which Richmond painted,[1] and which was reproduced in a well-known engraving. At first I think it disappointed people; this wasn't the gracious, winning countenance which they knew; it was more grave, even severe. But closer acquaintance, I think, showed that the painter had rightly caught and interpreted a quality of the face, of the man, and of his inward experiences. His was the freedom which comes through and after discipline, that of a man severe with himself behind his gentleness to others; yes, and with an unflinching sincerity in him which could not help bracing those with whom he had to do. Thus it was that both in his personality and in his teaching there was a blend of the strong austerity of the generation behind, and of the more expansive, lighter-hearted (and in many of us shallower-hearted) tone of the generation into which he lived on. Something of this was in Dr. Bright, his most intimate friend; in a deeper way still it had been anticipated in Dean Church, and was one cause of

[1] The original, at first given to Mrs. King, the bishop's mother, is now in the Common Room at Cuddesdon. It is reproduced at p. 55.

the extraordinary learning and persistent influence of one so retiring as the Dean. But (as you know, as we all know) in King it was King's. He did not suggest any one. Selfless as he was, there was no character with a more genuine outline and idiosyncrasy.

"What I have tried to say might be illustrated by his relation to Scott Holland, and the intrepid appeal which Holland made (with so much less response than it deserved) to the sons and grandsons of the Oxford Movement to bring its spiritual force to bear upon the problems, both intellectual and social, of a new time, or by his attitude to the question so delicate and complex about criticism and Scripture. But there was one development of Church life which all will unite to remember with gratitude. He felt how the renewed and deepened faith which had given new associations to the name of Oxford must prove itself in the great world, in the life of the nation, in the service of the Gospel; how the cords must be lengthened of a militant and evangelizing Church. He worked and taught steadily about 'Missions.' St. Stephen's House and the Oxford Mission to Calcutta remain as witnesses to the creative touch of his hand when he passed from among us (steering his way through a farewell meeting almost dangerously charged with emotion, by the 'Rub Lightly,' which had caught his eye on the match-box, sole remaining object in his dismantled study). We rejoiced with all our hearts that such a man should receive such an honour and have the great spiritual opportunities of a bishop entrusted to him; but we knew that Oxford would not see his like again, and we should hardly have been wrong if we had questioned whether in any other sphere he would be able to use influence as direct, as lovely, and so entirely timely as that of his Oxford professoriate. . . .

"Often have I inwardly used of him the words—'I had almost said even as they'—as those who doubted or fainted—'but then I should have condemned' what I had seen and known in him.

"Let me add two little instances which live in memory of the way in which he gave personal help. Walking at Cuddesdon, about the time of my ordination, we had spoken of the difficulties which beset faith. 'Well, you see,' he said, 'it's like this—I say to others, "The ice is thin, but I think we can get across.

I mean to try myself; won't you come along?"' About the same time, when we were about to open Keble College, speaking of our ideas of the kind of influence which we might use, he gave me the wise counsel, 'Don't try to Talbotize your men!'"

Future generations who have not known him will ask, "What was he like?" Study the portraits reproduced in this volume and then read what Canon Scott Holland has written. They represent the simple truth; there is no exaggeration in what he says. Every one who knew and loved him will endorse every word.

"A light went out of our lives when Edward King passed out of our companionship. It was a light that he carried with him—light that shone through him—light that flowed from him. The room was lit into which he entered. It was as if we had fallen under a streak of sunlight that flickered and danced and laughed and turned all to colour and to gold. Those eyes of his were an illumination. Even to recall him for an instant in the bare memory was enough to set all the day alive and glittering:

'My heart leaps up when I behold
A rainbow in the sky.'

So the heart leaped as it caught sight of that dear face that shone and quivered with the radiant hope that had made it its very own. Was there ever such a face? So gracious, so winning, so benignant, so tender? Its beauty was utterly natural and native. It made no effort to be striking, or marked, or peculiar, or special. It possessed just the typical beauty that should of right belong to the human countenance. It seemed to say, 'This is what a face is meant to be—this is the face that a man would have if he were really himself—this is the face that Love would normally wear.'

"We felt as if we had been waiting for such a face to come and meet us—a face that would simply reveal how deep is the goodness of which humanity is capable. . . .

"This gracious beauty of his countenance lasted to the very end. Indeed it had taken on a new charm; for the signals of old age in the wreathed wrinkles only gave an additional emphasis to the delicate rose-pink colouring of a face that was charged with the gaiety of an unconquerable gladness. . . . Those kindly eyes could indeed shine with a glint of steel;

and the level brows with their bushy eyebrows could wear a look of sternness; for he was a soldier at heart, and knew the stress of battle, and had a sword that he could wield. This touch of severity was apt to come out in photographs. But he was still an undying optimist. He believed in everything being for the best. He saw goodness and wisdom everywhere manifest. He loved everybody and every thing. He grew happier and happier. His eyes twinkled with dauntless merriment; his presence brimmed over with joy. After all the earth was a good place, and heaven would be better still. God be thanked."[1]

[1] *A Bundle of Memories*, p. 48.

CHAPTER V

FIRST YEARS OF THE EPISCOPATE: AIM AND OUTLOOK

Io ne parlo
Sì come dell' agricola, che Cristo
Elesse all' orto suo per aiutarlo.

Par. xii. 70–72.

I speak of him as of the labourer,
Whom Christ in His own garden chose to be
His help-mate.

Cary.

CHAPTER V

FIRST YEARS OF THE EPISCOPATE: AIM AND OUTLOOK

THERE were perhaps fewer forecasts as to Bishop Wordsworth's successor than usually happens when a vacancy occurs in the episcopate. It was a time when prophets were often at fault. A well-informed parish priest, with a large knowledge of the English clergy, spent some hours of a wintry day during a period of convalescence, in 1884, in the singular task of "removing" the diocesan bishops and making new appointments. A few years later he found that the only case in which he had come anywhere near the mark was in sending Dr. King to the See of Oxford. A postcard from Mr. Gladstone reached Lincoln at the end of January, 1885; and, although it did not mention any one by name, his correspondent clearly understood that Dr. King would very probably become Bishop of Lincoln. The offer was made on January 28th, and within a couple of days it was announced that the nomination had taken place. There was practically no delay in arriving at a decision. It was not that Edward King had anticipated or desired the appointment. Devotion to the will of God was the ruling principle of his life ; and so he had the gift of the pure in heart. We have seen it when he went to Cuddesdon, and again when he accepted the work at Oxford.

It would be almost possible to gather from his writings a series of maxims setting forth the whole *praxis* of spiritual and secular life as devotion to the will of God. He had always taught others to follow the lightest whispers of the divine will ; and, of course, as he said to his friends, he must try to do it himself. Perhaps in some ways it was not so difficult for him as it might have been for others. In spite of all the happiness he had found at Oxford the responsibilities of the Pastoral Professorship had always weighed heavily upon him. It was with real joy and delight, as his letters at the time witness, that he found himself called to what would really be, in a great agricultural diocese, the pastoral work he loved with his whole heart. So the call came, and he simply rose up and followed. It was the third week after Epiphany, and the *Christian Year*, his constant companion, seems to have been much in his mind, telling of the beauty of goodness often found in the lives of the poor and the power of their prayers. It recalled his Wheatley life and work. In letters to many friends he rejoices that he is to be a "bishop of the poor." He wrote as follows to Dr. Heurtley, Margaret Professor of Divinity and one of his brother canons of Christ Church :—

"CHRIST CHURCH, OXFORD,
"*Sunday*, *February*, 1885.

"MY DEAR DR. HEURTLEY,

"I must thank you, if only in a few words, for your very kind note and good wishes. You will believe me that I go to this new work with mingled feelings. I cannot help feeling the loss of my dear mother again very specially. We came in here together, and I feel that I go out alone; and I shall go to people who will never have known her, as so many here have done. But I am thankful for the opportunity of trying to carry out the high example of courage and trust which she always set me, and I think she would wish me to go.

"I have, as you know, no great gifts, but, by God's goodness, I have a great and real love of His poor; and, if it should please Him to let me be the bishop of His poor and enable me to help them to see more what they are to Him, and what He is to them, I think I shall be happy.

"I shall trust to your prayers for me—at least sometimes. I never can forget the kindness you and Mrs. Heurtley, and all your family, have shown to my dear mother and myself; nor can I thank you enough for the high example of your life. I shall be thankful if I can carry off with me some of that conscientious sense of duty and Christian courtesy which you have ever set before me so abundantly.

"Yours most gratefully and sincerely,

"EDWARD KING."

The Diocese of Lincoln had centres where wealth abounded, but it was an agricultural county, and English agriculture was passing through its lean years. It is not perhaps fanciful to read in line after line of the verses of the *Christian Year* for the third Sunday after Epiphany words that may have seemed to him to point to the new sphere of work, a home where instead of having to make a continual struggle on behalf of belief, the light of faith had found its way; where the light and music of nature filled the dull plains and fens; where Christian worth in simple homes would gladden the pastor's heart even in times of depression; where a great house of prayer and love and full harmonious praise stood "high above." All idealized, of course, but a happy coincidence, and he would delight in it.

The Consecration took place in St. Paul's Cathedral on the feast of St. Mark. The bishop-elect was presented by the Bishop of Oxford and the Bishop of Ely, two of his staunchest friends on the episcopal bench. The consecrating bishops were Archbishop Benson, Bishop Temple of London, Bishop Mackarness of Oxford, Bishop Woodford of Ely, Bishop Thorold of Rochester, Bishop Wilberforce of Newcastle, Bishop Trollope of Nottingham, Bishop Walsham How of Bedford, Bishop Boyd Carpenter of Ripon, and Bishop Bousfield of Pretoria. Dr. E. H. Bickersteth was at the same time consecrated to be Bishop of Exeter. There was, as the Primate characteristically noted in his diary, "a mighty congregation of the followers of the holy and influential Canon King."

Many had been the hopes and forecasts of his episcopate. Mr. Gladstone had spoken of the high expectations of the Diocese of Lincoln after the reign of Bishop Wordsworth, and his assurance that he could make no better provision to save disappointment than the nomination of Canon King. Canon Scott Holland had written in rapturous words, "It shall be a bishopric of love. The love of God behind, above, and about you! The love of the Blessed Spirit alive with good cheer within! The love of the poor shining from you." Dean Lake of Durham foretold an episcopate that would retain freshness and fervour of feeling in face of all difficulties. Bishop Wilkinson of Truro anticipated its spiritual power. Dr. Liddon, who was the preacher in St. Paul's, gathered the spirit of all these hopes in his sermon, "A Father in Christ."[1] It was a vindication of the office and work of a bishop in the Church of God. Much had happened during the three or four preceding years to

[1] *Clerical Life and Work*, p. 288.

lend special interest to a pronouncement on the subject by one who was the foremost living preacher in the English Church, whose sermons it was said filled Ludgate Hill with as great a crowd of people on Sunday as was found there on a weekday afternoon. Bishop Mackarness had, on appeal in the Courts, vindicated the right of the bishops to a veto in the case of proposed prosecutions in matters of ritual. Archbishop Tait, acting as a Father in God rather than as a Minister of State, had, on his deathbed, brought peace to the much harrassed and prosecuted Parish of St. Alban's, Holborn. The preacher himself had lately dedicated to Dr. King a volume of sermons,[1] in which he had expressed his opinion that the only hope of relief in the present Church troubles was to be found in the establishment of an Episcopal Court of Appeal for dealing with matters ecclesiastical. The powers vested or to be vested in the bishops formed one of the burning questions of the day. All this added largely to the importance of Dr. Liddon's sermon at the consecration. But it was when the preacher came to the personal aspect of his subject that

[1] *Church Troubles*, 1880.

he touched and thrilled the vast congregation in words that have been often quoted, and that perhaps no other could have so perfectly expressed. The bishops were Fathers in GOD. Such a relationship would depend on moral influences; on the respect inspired by firm and disinterested character; on the attraction exerted by a true love of GOD and man:—

"The eminent scholar and poet, not less saintly in his life than remarkable for his acquirements, who has lately left us, is to be succeeded in the See of St. Hugh by one whose nomination has thrilled the hearts of his brother Churchmen with the deepest thankfulness and joy. Never, probably, in our time has the great grace of sympathy, controlled and directed by a clear sense of the nature and sacredness of revealed truth, achieved so much among so many young men as has been achieved, first at the Theological College at Cuddesdon, and then from the Pastoral Chair at Oxford, in the case of my dear and honoured friend. He is surrounded at this solemn moment by hundreds who know and feel that to his care and patience, to his skill and courage, to his faith and spiritual insight, they owe all that is most precious in life and most certain to uphold them in the hour of death; and their sympathies and prayers are shared by many others who are absent from us in body, but present with us in spirit. Certainly, if past experience is any guarantee of what is to come, if there be such a thing as continuity of spiritual character and purpose, then we may hope to witness an episcopate which—κατὰ τὰς προαγούσας προφητείας—if current anticipations are not wholly at fault, will rank hereafter with those which in point of moral beauty stand highest on the roll of the later English Church—with Andrewes, with Ken, with Wilson, with Hamilton." [1]

The words were often recalled with joy and thankfulness in the Diocese of Lincoln. The bishop was a true father in God. He seldom claimed, even in his sermons, the relationship; but it was always there—bright, tender love and sympathy, and yet the firm strength of true fatherhood at the back; the heart always young, but, with it, the power and strength that made men trust him utterly. It was a day of almost unclouded brightness and happiness, and yet there were solemn and anxious thoughts in the bishop's mind. The

[1] *A Father in Christ*, p. 308.

appointment had called out fierce protests from the extreme wing of the Evangelicals, and the Church Association had tried to make trouble. So far all had gone well. Archbishop Benson's primacy promised to be a primacy of reconciliation. For a time troubles and difficulties might be ahead. There could be no compromise, no failure to uphold the truth, no treason to the Faith. It was St. Mark's Day, and the verses in the *Christian Year* must have had their message of hope and comfort. If disputes and divisions seem the inseparable lot of the Church in the world to-day, still—

> "On their tasks of love and praise
> The saints of GOD their several ways
> Right onward speed, yet join at last."

The enthronement of Bishop King as the sixty-second Bishop of the Diocese of Lincoln took place in the cathedral on Wednesday, May 19, 1885. Previous to the service the Corporation of the City of Lincoln presented an address to the bishop welcoming him on behalf of the citizens. The bishop, in his reply, thanked the members of the corporation, and the city magistrates who accompanied them, for their kindly words of welcome, and said

Dr. King (about 1885).

(From photo by S. Walker taken soon after the Bishop s Consecration.)

Page 104.

that it was his most earnest desire in coming to dwell amongst them to join with them in all efforts for the increased welfare of the city and diocese.

A great congregation assembled in the cathedral. The service was a celebration of the Holy Communion, at which the bishop celebrated for the first time in his cathedral church. After the Creed he delivered an address from the sanctuary-steps. Words and phrases that soon became familiar throughout the diocese made here their first appearance. Man's lost happiness could only be regained in fellowship with God. To bring man back again to Himself had been the one purpose of all God's dealings with humanity under the Old Dispensation. It had been made possible by the Incarnation of the Son of God, and was being carried on in the Church He had founded upon earth. It was the bishop's joy and responsibility to be called to share that work in the Diocese of Lincoln, and to ask all, clergy and laity alike, to share that happiness and responsibility with him. They were old and familiar lines of thought, but there was something in the personality of the speaker that gave a new power and force to the message.

Everybody felt it. Sentence after sentence, fresh and crisp and clear-cut and appealing, spoken in quietness and simplicity and without any apparent effort, came home to every one in the congregation. There was the simple and fearless expression of his own mind and experience, intensely personal, and yet without the slightest trace of self-assertion. It was one of his special gifts, one of the gifts bestowed so sparingly in the world to-day. It was all perfectly and entirely natural—his gratitude, his trust, his joy and aspiration, his refreshment, his plans for the future, his hope that many of his hearers who lived at a distance would share his hospitality and the refreshment of the cathedral, his sense of divergent thoughts which might exist but must never make separations, his trust and reliance on their prayers. Every one was drawn to him. Here are one or two characteristic sentences from the address :—

"The same spirit of selfish individualism which separated man from God makes man self-willed and separates him from his fellows."

"It is the great work of God to bring man back again to Himself and into loving communion with his fellow men."

"Christ came to reconcile man to God, and man to man, and in time to remove the curse from Nature, and to bring into closer communion man and Nature, man and man, man and God.

"It is our great privilege, yours and mine, to share in this work of reconciliation, so that in God man may find that fullness of rest which apart from Him he cannot find—rest of the mind in knowing the truth, rest of the heart in coming nearer to the personal God in knowledge and love."

"Let there be a right emulation to see who can be quickest to find, who strongest to carry back, who most brilliant to rejoice in the joy that the lost is found."

In the afternoon an address of welcome, signed by four hundred and seventy-nine clergy of the diocese, was presented to the bishop by the Bishop-Suffragan of Nottingham, supported by Canon Wilde and Canon Perry, the proctors in Convocation.

In his reply the bishop said, "My first words must be words of thanksgiving to Almighty God for His unspeakable goodness in granting me the place of a chief pastor in

His holy Church." Then followed words of gratitude to the clergy for their "loyal but too kindly-worded address," and one of those sincere and gracious references to his predecessor, Bishop Wordsworth, which were so frequently on his lips during the first years of his episcopate: "I know that under God I owe this loyalty and kindness almost entirely to the example and teaching of him whom not only this diocese, but all true English Churchmen everywhere, revere and love, my great predecessor, in whose well-marked footsteps it will be my great desire to tread." And then, after speaking of the work of the bishop and clergy as St. Paul describes it, "to present every man perfect in Christ Jesus," came one of those simple and moving references which now and again broke through the spirit of Tractarian reserve that nearly always kept inner life and personal experience in the background:—

"I am not very old yet in years, but I have known enough of bodily and mental suffering, both in myself and in others, to be separated, I trust, for ever from the allurements and ambitions of the world. My only reason for coming among you is to do God's will and to help others to find out the will of God as it is made known to us in Christ and by Christ in His Church; that in Christ we may all draw nearer to God and to each other." Here, as one of his friends used to say, was the secret of his untroubled and undisturbed calm in years to come, whatever tributes of praise or words of censure were passed on him. "Let me beg of you to give me forbearance and patience in your judgement of my words and actions, even when we agree; and, when we differ, at least to give me credit for disinterested sincerity." The bishop ended with the expression of a fervent hope that a real personal friendship might soon spring up between the clergy and himself.

It had been a great and wonderful day for the bishop, and really for the diocese. Links of friendship and sympathy had been formed which augured well for the future. The bishop and his clergy knew and trusted one another, and the trust grew and increased as, month by month and year by year, it became more evident that the episcopate of Bishop King was not a ministry of controversy, but always and everywhere a ministry of pastoral love and sympathy. He had a full and definite Gospel to preach, and he delivered it fully and simply everywhere —in the cathedral, in great town churches, in the villages, in retreats, in quiet days, at Confirmations—the Gospel of the grace of God, manifested in the Incarnation of His Son, and coming with the fullness of the blessing of Christ in His holy Church.

One who knew the bishop in the early days of his episcopate writes: "I wonder whether I dare try to write reminiscences of the days when he first found himself in Lincoln and began to settle down there. It was all very different from the Oxford life; and yet there was the cathedral with its great broad tower and its memories of great bishops in the past; and its promises and possibilities of the future; and the Old Palace where bishops had lived in the past, and where his house was to be built before so very long. It was at first, perhaps, rather a lonely life, yet with glimpses of the past coming into it. There were all kinds of earnest and good people round him, but he was hardly yet one of them. He had visions of what might be, but he often lived in what had been. Great memories of the past, in which he felt he had, if a small, a very real part, pressed on him —Pusey and Keble and Marriott, and all the great Tractarian traditions. He had been, at any rate, a disciple. It was a background of life, a world into which it was possible to withdraw, from which there came streams of strengthening and steadying influence. New days and new thoughts were ahead, and he had to guide a Church in the midst of them. Many, half the world over, men who had formed his spiritual household at Cuddesdon or at Oxford, would look to him for guidance and direction.

"And then there was the smaller world—the Lincolnshire world—that was to be his first care. It was so different from the surroundings of the last twenty years, so much simpler in a way, and yet with its own complex problems and manifold interests. Perhaps he hardly realized it himself, but in those first days and afterwards he was in a special sense a bishop of the whole English Church, and not merely Bishop of Lincoln. And yet Lincoln and Lincolnshire were his last great gift from his Lord. And it all appealed to him so wonderfully. At Oxford there had of late years been always the terrible task of holding the fortress of belief in God. It had sometimes seemed in absolute danger. The sixties and seventies had been years of immense strain. Here it was different. There was, at any rate, the simple belief in God. It gladdened and helped him, and brought increasing brightness and happiness into his life. It was something to build on. There was hope of bringing the blessings of the Church to the people, even the poorest. Bishop Wordsworth had laid a strong foundation, and he was called to build upon it. In somewhat later days there was the perpetual call and inspiration of the busy city below the hill. It was pleasant on a summer evening, sauntering up and down the terrace of the Old Palace garden, looking over the city to the hill beyond ; but "life is not made to loiter on terraces," he used to say. The city, the foundries, the great chimneys, the buzzers calling the men to work, were perpetual inspirations. The men in the streets, the surging crowd at half-past twelve going to dinner, the bright faces, the eager energy, the rapid talk, the children meeting their fathers—how it all touched him. It made him long to win them to the fullness of the Faith. An opportunity soon offered, and he told them what was in his heart. It was at a gathering of foundry men in one of the mess-rooms for the inauguration of the Winter Session of the Chancellor's Night Schools. When it came to him to speak he told the men of the love for Lincoln that was growing in his heart, and—to their immense amazement—of the prayers he prayed for them every morning when he heard them pass on their way to work under his window at Hilton House. The cheer with which they burst in upon his words was the proof and pledge of the friendship they offered him, and which, through all his years at Lincoln, was one of the great happinesses of his life."

Instead of waiting the usual three years, Bishop King held his Primary Visitation in October, 1886, after he had been eighteen months in the diocese. It was written with great thought and care, chiefly during a summer holiday at Buxton. He had gained, it is evident from the contents of the charge, a full and sufficient knowledge of the circumstances of the diocese ; and he was anxious to make the delivery of his primary charge to the clergy and churchwardens an opportunity for putting forward as fully and clearly as possible what he felt to be the aim and purpose of his episcopate.

It is the nearest approach to a piece of constructive theological work that Bishop King ever undertook. It was often thought that he might some day write a great book on Christian Ethics; but the demands upon his time and powers soon made it evident that such a task could never be undertaken. This must be the reason for dealing in some detail with the charge and the circumstances of its preparation and delivery. He had entered with fullest sympathy into the work of the Church in the diocese with his extraordinary power of seeing the best everywhere, and judging rather by what was being aimed at than by what was being actually accomplished. He had visited a very large number of parishes, and made hosts of friends. His frank sincerity and his enthusiastic love of goodness had largely disarmed any lingering suspicions or opposition. Some of the odd and amusing stories of these days are *ben trovato*, though they may have had no other foundation. His meeting, for instance, on a station platform a clergyman who was generally supposed to be in many ways fiercely opposed to the new bishop : "They tell me you are my greatest opponent in Lincolnshire. I am sure we shall be good friends when we get to know one another"; or the merry twinkle of his eye when a severe Evangelical layman, who was on some public occasion entertaining him at luncheon with the chilliest of exact courtesy, passed the salt to the bishop: "We *must* be friends now that we have eaten salt together."

The Confirmations had brought him into touch with the young men and girls and children of the diocese, of whom he had confirmed more than five thousand. A number of new churches had been consecrated, and he had seen the diocesan organizations and their committees at work. There was much that gave grounds of hope. "Of all the answers to my visitation questions there is only one instance in which definite unbelief is mentioned. In the main our people are believers in God and in our Lord Jesus Christ; they are baptized; they hold to the Bible; they are frequent in prayer and praise. Truly in all this there is matter for great thankfulness and hope." "I do not gather from the visitation returns that actual godlessness is as prevalent amongst us as I have sometimes feared."[1] It must be borne in mind that in 1886 Lincolnshire was much more outside the main current of English thought and experience than it is to-day. There were no really large towns, and the majority of the people lived quiet lives in the country with a steady, if not altogether enthusiastic, respect for the traditional religion of the countryside.

The form and contents of the charge clearly show how much all this had impressed the writer. He begins by taking it for granted that faith in God and respect for a Christian standard of life are more or less to be found everywhere; and while he urges that definite teaching is necessary to make these things secure, he feels able to build upon them the great work he was convinced he had been sent to Lincoln to accomplish—"To bring home to the people, and especially to the poor, the blessings of the Church." The expression occurs time after time in the charge. It shows clearly and distinctly the bishop's mind as to the great aim and purpose of his episcopate; "What is the special work, then, which God has called me to do? If I am not too presumptuous in speaking so definitely of myself

[1] p. 79.

in relation to God I will say, I hope, if it be His will, that my work may be to bring home to the hearts of the people, and especially of the poor, the blessings of the Church." "It seems to me that to this point God has been bringing us during these last thirty years. The very foundations of the Faith have been assailed; but, thanks be to God, they stand for many of us firmer than before, or rather we stand firmer in our relation to them."

The bishop is emphatic in the expression of his conviction that Faith in God can only attain its full measure in the Church, and that Christian character can only be perfected in the power of the Holy Spirit and by graces ministered through the Church of Christ.

There is, of course, much in the charge that is now perfectly familiar to all Church people. The bishop deals at length with difficulties which were often encountered in teaching the doctrine of the Holy Catholic Church, and the remedies he proposed to meet them. He had received his own deepest religious experience in the days when a vivid faith in the Church was almost a new thing for English people. It had been bound up for him with the deepest and best things of his spiritual life. At times, perhaps, even with his extraordinary gift of intellectual and spiritual sympathy, he found it difficult to understand the coldness and indifference, and even prejudice and suspicion, with which so many people regarded this Article of the Apostles' Creed.

But although there is much that is quite familiar in the bishop's exposition of his subject, there is one passage which must be quoted at length, and which may almost be said to be his own contribution to the doctrine of the Church :—

"Another more subtle difficulty lies in the apparent paradox in the use of media. The soul is jealous of any interference between itself and God. Possessing powers for the enjoyment through eternity of the unveiled vision of God, the soul is impatient of the mediatorial kingdom ; it feels the restraint of times and places and persons ; it longs for the Communion with God and with the saints in heaven, where the Lord is the Temple. This fear of interference between the soul and its God makes the soul jealous of Sacraments, of Priesthood, of Creeds, of a Church, even in some cases of a Bible.

"This jealousy for union with God is worthy of the greatest respect and consideration, for it speaks of a great past, and is a pledge of a still greater future. But it needs fatherly instruction and correction. We are on our way back again to God, but it is as those who have fallen from God, and we need the discipline of times and places and persons, if we are to inherit the fullness of the freedom that is prepared for us, and to follow the Lamb whithersoever He goeth. We need to consider the apparent paradox that by separation and limitation God is reconciling the world back again to Himself. God loved all the world, yet He chose one nation to be His own; God loved the chosen people, but He chose one particular tribe to minister in holy things. He loved all the sons of Levi, but chose the family of Aaron to be His priests. God was in all the world, yet He chose Jerusalem to be the city where He would dwell. In the language of Scripture, 'God deviseth means that His banished be not expelled from Him.'" [1]

It is, as Bishop Magee ("who, of all the bishops at that time on the bench, possessed

[1] 2 Sam. xiv. 14.

the acutest and most vigorous intellect")[1] wrote at the time, "a thought which runs out very far and very deep under all our Christian life. The *im*patient instead of the 'patient waiting for Christ' is seen, when we come to think of it, to be the source of no small part of our ecclesiastical and even our personal errors and troubles."

Extraordinary changes passed over English national life as well as over English religious life between 1829, the year Edward King was born, and 1910, the year he died. The England in which he grew to manhood was almost beyond description different from the England of his episcopate. In 1829 the population of the country was under twelve millions, in 1910 it was close on forty millions. It was the era of the growth of the great towns and great centres of population. At its beginning the Church seemed effete, worn out, useless; at its end, it had passed through strange and marvellous revivals, and was once more upon its trial, facing a new world with new challenges and new perils. Edward King lived his life of

[1] Bishop King's sermon at Peterborough after Archbishop Magee's funeral.

eighty years through it all. He had in some degree faced and measured it, and he had without dispute left a real mark upon the religious life of his times. He would have said, and of course it is true, that he had only a share in what a large number of men were engaged in doing; but his influence was, perhaps, more widespread than that of most of them.

The Oxford Movement had brought the claims and powers of the Church to the front again. Its leaders were men of calm and studious lives, only thrust into prominence by unwelcome controversies and persecutions. The movement was at first an appeal to the clergy, but it soon began to feel its way into the towns. It was hopeless to expect that a clergy trained, or rather untrained, as the English clergy had for the most part been, could cope with the spiritual needs of the great masses of the people gathered in the growing towns and cities of the land.

It was the beginning of the problem which almost overwhelms the Church to-day. The clergy need to be trained, and the twenty-five years of Edward King's life that followed his ordination were devoted with marvellous success to a share in this great work at Cuddesdon and Oxford. Previous chapters have attempted to give some idea of his influence in training and moulding men for work in the large town parishes. He lived and worked quietly in the background, but the work told. It had a simplicity and intensity which sprang from a heart aflame with pastoral love, and passionately interested in human life and character.

The episcopate gave him the opportunity of bringing the same influence into the villages and towns of Lincolnshire. It would be interesting indeed if he had kept a diary of thoughts and hopes and impressions, something that would have shown the secrets of his inner life. Nothing of the kind has been found among his papers. If he ever made such notes he must have deliberately destroyed them. Perhaps he felt that his whole outlook on life and the world was too simple to commit to writing. He used laughingly to say that he had only four or five sermons, and that his chief perplexity was to find fresh collars and cuffs for them. He meant that "one thing was needful." Perhaps too he felt, as so many others have felt these last forty years, that the changing circumstances and claims of life were demanding, not, perhaps, so much new statements of the Faith—that is one and unchanging—as ever-new applications of its claims to guide and direct souls in the manifold intricacies of daily life and conduct. There has, however, been found a short but touching and interesting fragment, in which the bishop, during a few quiet hours at the beginning of a holiday in 1887, set down in one of his sermon note-books some thoughts on his own life at that time, and his hopes and plans for the future. The notes are fragmentary and incomplete, but they are, perhaps for that very reason, the more interesting.

They are, so far as they go, a sketch and outline of thoughts and plans which occupied his mind throughout his episcopate. They were written on his mother's birthday. He is just starting for his holiday abroad, and the date is :—

"PAVILION, FOLKESTONE,
"*Aug.* 21, 1887.

"Ah ! what do I not owe to this day, my dearest mother's birthday !

"I fear of late I have sadly fallen from her bright example. Her brightness and unselfish cheerfulness in making others happy even in her own broken widowed life at Cuddesdon and at Oxford. How was it? Not by crushing out the family life and love which remained, but by a singular continuance of her own life encircled in its own peculiar communion with God—by the continuing sense of duty which pervaded her life—religious, domestic, social. Her devotions, attendance at church, devotional reading, etc., household duties, family letters—keeping the family together—letters on business, presents, visits, calling on neighbours—all this was done on a principle of duty which gave her a peculiar independent satisfaction, and left upon others a sense of strength and brightness which was most refreshing and invigorating.

"And how am I to follow this?

"Only as she did, by God's help.

"By maintaining my own communion with Him in the midst of all my work—St. Bernard's *Vacare Considerationi*.[1]

"Communion implies union of the thought and conscience, regulated human will with the divine will.

. . . .

"By study.

"Where am I?

[1] "Get time to think," as the bishop often quoted it.

"Thank God, more restful than I once was. How can I be thankful enough for Cuddesdon and Oxford? Most wonderfully God has answered my indefinite desire.

"The Catholic Faith, *D.G.*, I never doubted; only, may God give me grace to see His truth with sufficient clearness to know and do His will.

"The basis of ethics, and the characteristics of heathen and Christian ethics, *D.G.*, Oxford made clear to me and more strong than ever.

"(α) Personality.

"(β) Responsibility.

"(γ) Freedom.

"(δ) Power.

"(ϵ) Duty.

"Personal ethics send me to social ethics.

"Man finds his individual perfection in the State, with the aid of external law.

"This brings me to where I am, and points to two considerations and lines of future study.

"The Catholic Church, as the one state or city of God in which man, through the supernatural assistance provided for him and in the Communion of Saints, finds his highest individual perfection and happiness in the love of God and of his neighbour.

"'Fecisti nos ad Te, Domine,' etc.

"I must read the history of England generally; give especial attention to the constitutional development, the history of the growth of our constitution.

"This I ought to do to understand the indefinite national sentiment which strongly influences people of very different degrees of knowledge.

"This I ought to do to fit myself, if it please God, for any opportunities of work which may come to me in the House of Lords.

"This I ought to do in order that I may help the people not to lose the high ethical opportunities offered them in different kinds of *local government*—parochial, county, etc.; regarding such systems as opportunities for united exercises of social, political, national life.

"This I ought to do to fit myself for the work in Convocation, so as to remove as far as possible all needless antagonism between true national loyalty and the extra-national duties to the Church.

"I must try to arrange a course of English history in different groups.

"I must study the Catholic Church. Thank God, not for myself, but to see how I may bring it home to the hearts of the people.

"Dissent is wrong and ought not to be.

"A divided Christendom is wrong, and ought not to be." [1]

. . . .

[1] S. John xvii.

CHAPTER VI

THE BISHOP AT HOME

La lor concordia e i lor lieti sembianti
Amore e maraviglia e dolce sguardo
Faceano esser cagion di pensier santi.

Par. xi. 76–78.

Their concord and glad looks, wonder and love,
And sweet regard gave birth to holy thoughts.

Cary.

CHAPTER VI

THE BISHOP AT HOME

FOR many years the Bishops of Lincoln had lived at Riseholme—a large country house with somewhat extensive grounds, three miles away from the station at Lincoln. It was in many ways an inconvenient and unsatisfactory arrangement. Bishop King was anxious to live nearer the cathedral, and in a house which would be more accessible to people who wished to see him. The Diocese of Lincoln covers a very large area. Parts of it are a great distance from the cathedral city, and the railway communications are such as make a journey to Lincoln a whole day's business; in many places the clergy live miles away from a station. The Old Palace, which, in the thirteenth or fourteenth century, had been the residence of the bishops, was in absolute ruin. In the seventeenth and eighteenth centuries it had practically been used as a stone-quarry when repairs were needed at the cathedral. It was impossible to restore the ruins, but the architect to the Ecclesiastical Commissioners designed a large and useful house, which was built in 1887 as an enlargement of a house which had stood in the Old Palace grounds since 1737. It stands on the hill-side, and from its south front commands a striking view of the city and the open country beyond. The cathedral stands on the highest level of the hill, and the Palace-grounds occupy three levels or terraces below—one where the north front of the house and the chief entrance are found; a second from which the south front has been built up facing a moderate-sized lawn and garden, with a few good trees, and having the Palace ruins to the left; and a still lower third level, with tennis-lawns and gardens. Although there are other houses on nearly all sides, the Palace stands in a fairly retired position, and can hardly be seen from any part of the city, built as it is on various levels and dominated by the cathedral in the background.

The chapel has been built by an ingenious use of a portion of the Old Palace ruins. It is connected with the house by a picturesque, but not very convenient, corridor; but the chapel itself, designed by Mr. G. F. Bodley, is worthy

Front of the Old Palace, Lincoln.

(Showing the study windows with the drawing-room windows above them. On the right is the chapel.)

Page 132.

of its place and position. It is very lofty, and has a stately altar and sanctuary; and there is an admirably-designed oak screen, with stalls, at the west end. The east window is high up over a canopied dossal, and has lights illustrating the Annunciation, the Nativity, and the Crucifixion, with figures of St. Remigius, St. Hugh, St. Christopher, and St. Edward, the two last as being patrons of Bishop Wordsworth and Bishop King. The entire furnishing and decoration of the chapel was undertaken by members of the English Church Union, in response to an appeal made by the President of the Society. The consecration took place in 1888. In his letter of thanks to Lord Halifax the bishop, after an expression of personal gratitude, wrote in words which have been often called to mind:—

"And yet the real pleasure of the kindness is not simply personal, but rather the reverse. The real ground for rejoicing at this great act of kindness is surely this—that it shows how grateful people are for the sacramental blessings of the Church. . . . It has been the great and undeserved privilege of my life to have had friends amongst (what is called) all classes of society; from your lordship to one (of whom I felt quite unworthy) who died in gaol; and I know, by a blessed experience, what the heart of a man is when in sacramental union with his God.

"The real want of England is to make English hearts happy with the happiness for which God made them what they are. Money, rank, political power—these are well enough, and should be given to men as God may direct, in His own time and in His own way. But the real want of England is to know the peace and blessedness of the love of God and the love of man in the sacramental life of Christ."

The chapel was in constant use. Here the bishop celebrated daily—when he did not celebrate himself he always communicated (when he could) every day. Even at the very end of his life, when ill, he would say, "I must get up if I can but crawl down to the celebration." Here institutions to benefices often took place, and assistant curates were licensed. Private Confirmations were not seldom held here, and occasionally the bishop ordained in the chapel. At Ember seasons it was, of course, used all day.

Opening out of the chapel itself was a good-sized sacristy, which contained a very small

The Bishop's Private Chapel at the Old Palace.

age 134.

portable altar which had belonged to Dr. Pusey, and which the bishop had used for two years at Hilton House before the Old Palace was ready for him. There was a chasuble of Dr. Pusey's, which he had apparently used at this little altar. Turning to the house, the big drawing-room, with its magnificent view overlooking the city, contained portraits of Bishops Wordsworth, Jackson, and Kaye, and pictures of Bishop King's mother and of his soldier brother who was killed in the Crimea. In the dining-room Bishop Sanderson's portrait was given the place of honour over the chimneypiece; the bishop was very insistent on this, and used constantly to point it out to visitors.

In the entrance-hall there were views of Wheatley, Cuddesdon, and Christ Church—an illustrated epitome of the bishop's career. Opening into the hall was the bishop's study, the room in which he habitually lived. "It was here," writes one who knew well the inner life of the Old Palace, "that the honey was stored, all the other rooms were more or less empty cells." It was a large, well-proportioned room, almost all the furniture of which was the gift of friends. Two great windows looked over the city, which lay below the terraced gardens and the houses just beyond. Bookcases full and overflowing ran round two sides, and there was a grate at the far end where the fire seemed always to burn brightly. The bishop loved warmth—fire in the winter and the sunshine that filled the room in summer, for it faced due south. Books and papers and pamphlets littered a large desk which stood where the light from one of the windows fell sideways upon it, and the warmth of the fire reached it easily. A sofa piled up with books, mostly new volumes of theology, was near the window. On an easel in the middle of the room was a striking portrait of Sailer, formerly Bishop of Ratisbon. His works in forty-two volumes on a shelf of the book-case near at hand had been for years, since Dr. Döllinger had first introduced them to the bishop, in frequent use for reference.

A massive oak writing-table, which had been a present from Cuddesdon students, stood in the centre of the room ; this was always littered with letters and papers and books and writing-paper ; but, standing on it amid all the apparent confusion, there could always be seen a small mother-of-pearl crucifix (which had belonged to Dr. Pusey), and a photograph of Dean Church.

A corner of Dr. King's Study at the Old Palace.

Page 136.

On the prayer desk were Dr. Pusey's book of private prayers, and Dr. Bright's *Ancient Collects*. On a little table close by his arm-chair, and on one side of the fireplace, there was a miniature of the bishop's mother, with a small vase of flowers always in front of it. On the wall close by hung a picture of Dr. Pusey, a photograph from a sketch made when he was preaching; and also one of the doctor's study.

Over the chimneypiece hung the Arundel reproduction of Perugino's "Crucifixion," and on one side of it, framed, was the word Κόπος ("labour"), which had been suggested by Bishop Wilberforce's life of untiring energy. On either side of the fireplace were two book-cases, mostly filled with French and German theological books, except one corner which was reserved for his books on Dante. On one of these book-cases stood an oil-paining of St. Hugh, which was the work of the Rev. Canon Frederick Sutton, Rector of Brant Broughton. Elsewhere on the walls were to be seen portraits of Bishop Wilberforce and Charles Marriott, and above the door a picture of "Bethel." [1] On a table close to the sofa stood a beautiful engraving of Millet's *Angelus*,

[1] See p. 69.

which Francis Paget, his successor in the Pastoral Chair at Oxford, had given to the bishop, who loved the devotion expressed in the picture as suggesting ideals which he hoped that the farm lads and girls in the Fens might one day reach.

In the great bow-window, on the construction of which the bishop had insisted (it was not in the original design of the Ecclesiastical Commissioners' architect), stood a straight-backed, tall, grandfather's arm-chair, the gift of his dear friends Mr. and Mrs. T. M. Kitchin. Here the bishop constantly sat in summer as he worked at his letters, looking up from time to time to watch the birds on the lawn, or to look across the houses and high chimneys of Lincoln to Canwick Hill. On the chimney-piece itself were two oak goblets carved from the timber of a tree which had formerly stood in the north-east corner of the Minster Yard. Here too was an ostrich-egg, which had been given to the bishop by the blacksmith at Wheatley, and a small wooden box, which a carpenter in the parish had presented to him when he left. The bishop delighted in showing this to his friends as an example of *completeness*, quoting as he did so the words of the donor,

"I knew you would like it, sir, because it is the same on each side." It was an exact square.

There was an atmosphere in the room—a sense of faith, devotion, sympathy, friendliness. "It was really a home room," one writes; "it was always a happiness to find the bishop there as he rose from his chair to meet you. It all fitted in, so to speak—the purple cassock, the pectoral cross, the friendly look, the bright word of welcome, the warm grasp of the hand. There might have been nothing else that mattered but you and what you had come for; and really for the time there was not; unless, perhaps, he was tired or had some anxious business on hand, and a strained look came over his face, and you tried to get away without letting him know you had seen it." It was a home, and not a business or committee-room. Papers and letters were often, it must be admitted, in much confusion, and it was not always easy for the bishop or his chaplain to put hands at a moment's notice on a letter or a paper needed for reference. A hunted and troubled look would come over his face, but at last it was sure to turn up, and some happy word of apology and self-depreciation put every one at ease.

People came on many different errands, and never really in vain; they might not get exactly what they sought, but they found the keen interest, the sympathy, the wise counsel, the strong guidance and direction, the delight of the visit, the things that really counted and helped and mattered. The bishop was almost too accessible; but he had once, when an undergraduate, learnt a lesson from Charles Marriott, and he never forgot it. He had gone one day into Marriott's room at Oriel and, finding him apparently absorbed in work, was leaving with an apology, when he was called back: "What is it, King?" "I will come another time, sir; you are too busy." And then came the lesson: "Do you know what 'being busy' means? If what you want is of more importance to you than what I am at is to me, I am not busy. What is it, King?" The bishop always remembered it, and he used to tell the story with much glee. Yet he had ways of avoiding the too frequent visits of people who were, perhaps, ready to take advantage of his open doors; and he knew how to bring a useless interview to a close so easily that the greatest bore could hardly feel injured.

Perhaps he was not a great student in his

later years. He had read much of his own subjects, and also of other things at Cuddesdon and Oxford. He knew the Faith. He knew what Christian Ethics stood for. Now he was the scribe instructed unto the kingdom of heaven, who had to bring forth out of his treasures things new and old. Those books had largely served their purpose. There were three or four thousand volumes, and amongst them the great tomes of the Fathers, Dr. Pusey's books, Dr. Liddon's volumes of sermons, marked and marked again ; the Dante books ; Bishop Butler in Mr. Gladstone's famous edition ; a large and curious assortment of bishops' charges and pastorals — he was an inveterate reader of these at home and abroad ; some, perhaps unexpected, volumes of Archbishop Magee, greatly treasured, "the most reasonable of all reasoners," as he said in the sermon he preached at Peterborough after the archbishop's funeral ; a large assortment of French and German and Italian theology— volumes often evidently just bought and read and marked for a certain purpose and then laid aside ; a special basket for the latest French and Italian pastorals, notably those of the Bishop of Cremona, Geremia Bonomelli, with whom he had slight but happy ties of friendship; a certain number of books dealing with Higher Criticism—a line of study he regarded with anxious interest but with little real sympathy. Charles Marriott had taught him that "the utmost criticism can do is to prepare a correct text for the reading of the spiritual eye"—a maxim he often quoted. The books were there, the books of the great leaders he had known in the past, the men whose influence lived within him.

And the books too of the younger men. They were read and marked often most carefully—the primary charge of a new bishop, a study by an old Cuddesdon man, a new formulation of ethics, a passing pamphlet. There they were, often with a note of query in the margin, read probably on a railway journey—to judge by the shaky lines of the markings—or in the early morning after a wakeful night. He got out of them what was best, what was of use to him. There are books which are friends and others which are the craftsman's tools. He had both—Dante and Butler and Wordsworth among the first, and always the *Christian Year*. They had served him well. He knew the great passages that had found and helped him. He was a teacher of the Faith that was in him, not an echo of other men's thoughts—a disciple, but a "disciple" (like Marriott) with an independent mind.[1] He had no desire to restate the Faith for the modern world; but he had an intense and almost passionate desire to state Christian ethics in the language of the day, in words easy to be understood by the simplest people—and he often went great lengths in doing so.

The Faith was one; but the fruits of the Faith in life and conduct were manifold as the individual life of humanity. It was this that gave such steadiness and strength, and, at the same time, such delight and appeal to his sermons. You always knew the Faith—almost the very words in which he would express it. You never knew, and never could know beforehand, the new and manifold ways in which he would appeal for the expression of that Faith in human life. The Faith was one; the life was manifold; and it was the Faith that made possible and certain the life and conduct.

"Yes," a busy woman once said; "Yes, as

[1] See Dean Church, *Oxford Movement*, p. 88.

soon as I saw him in the pulpit, I felt I wanted to be good, and I knew I could be."

When at home, as has been said, the bishop would celebrate the Holy Eucharist [1] in his own chapel every day about 8.15 o'clock. Family prayers followed, and then breakfast at 9 o'clock. A little before 10 o'clock, if he were not going out in the diocese, he would retire to his study and begin his letters. At 10.30 he would say his office [2] with his chaplain, and at 11 o'clock he was ready to receive his secretary—Mr. W. W. Smith, on whose constant and wise help the bishop relied with absolute trust. The morning passed in interviews and writing. "Accessibility" was one of the mottoes of his life; and no one who came to see him would fail to be asked to luncheon, so that he almost always had some guests with him at that time; while, on market-days, his table would be crowded, as

[1] He always wore the Eucharistic vestments, generally white ones, except on great festivals. "For twenty years, within a few days, I have worn them [i.e. the vestments] as a rule every day in my private chapel."—*Charge*, 1907, p. 64.

[2] He never missed saying his office. It was very often said in the train; and, if starting on a journey in the morning before he had had time to say it, he would not open the newspaper until he had recited Matins.

The Bishop's Throne, Lincoln Cathedral.

(*From a photo by S. Smith.*)

Page 145.

the more frequent trains into Lincoln made it easier for the clergy and others to come and see him then. It was not often that he could get out after luncheon; but, when he could do so, he went for a short walk, always coming back in time to attend Evensong in the cathedral at 4 o'clock. After that he would go back straight to his study and go on with his letters or other work, a cup of tea being brought to him as he wrote—for no man was ever more free from the thraldom of 5 o'clock tea; and he very seldom was known to have more than one cup of tea and a slice of bread and butter at this meal. At 7.30 came dinner, and afterwards he would sit alone in his arm-chair and read. At 10 o'clock he had prayers in chapel, after which he would read or write till nearly 11, and then bed.

But it was in reality only quite seldom that he spent the whole day at home. He was constantly out in the diocese, and the more he could visit the small country parishes the happier he was. He delighted in anything which took him amongst the country people; he revelled in harvest festivals, for they gave him an opportunity of speaking to many who were not always in church at other times.

It must not be supposed that the bishop had any special purpose in view when people were asked to luncheon or dinner, any diocesan or other business purpose, neither was it done simply as an act of deliberate kindness. There was, so to say, no conscious effort about it. It was all a matter of happy friendship and delight in people and things and social intercourse. It was a real refreshment to him, although of course there were times of exception. His house, his table, flowers, garden, peacocks, fantail-pigeons were a simple delight to him; and he loved to have people to share things with him. He sat and talked and listened and learnt and laughed and wondered, and was perfectly happy. At times, when some trouble, or sorrow, or wrong, or sin was mentioned, his face grew grave, and the lines marked themselves more deeply. It was bound to be so, for he, more than most men, realized what Wordsworth meant by "the burthen of the mystery, the heavy and the weary weight of all this unintelligible world." He lived *in viâ*; it was only *in patriâ*, that it would be lightened. And yet it was never allowed to gloom or darken times of refreshing and happy social life. The bishop was an admirable talker, but he never aimed at being a *raconteur*; and he certainly never reached the "years of anecdotage."

His interests were interests of the present; the things that were happening day by day; the things he had seen and delighted in; the methods, perhaps, at times of pastoral life, but these only when a number of clergy were gathered round him. He had no axes to grind, no desire to "improve the occasion," no mission to preach in social life. Sermons had their place elsewhere. He looked rather for the surprises and delights of social intercourse, and he always found them. He never seemed bored unless, perhaps, a man began to talk in a too self-satisfied way about his work and its success. At times reminiscences of friends and people he had known in the past dropped out; but unless he happened to be with some one who had shared them, or unless some special appeal was made to him, he did not seem to care to talk about such things. They were many of them too deep and serious a part of his life and experience; or if they were unpleasant, or things that involved criticism, or matters of a controversial nature, he was not anxious to recall them. He had had no small part in some of the "Church troubles" of the past, but it was on the rarest occasions that he referred to them. Had he written any pages of autobiography, such matters as the Lincoln Trial would hardly have appeared. He was always easy and happy in conversation, and he had a great gift of expressing his thoughts in perfectly worded phrases, which dropped so naturally from his lips, that for the most part people simply enjoyed them and hardly realized the intellectual power and large experience of life and thought that must have gone to make them such easy possibilities of ordinary conversation. He was a perfect host at a dinner party, and thoroughly enjoyed either large or small gatherings of people at such times. He is credited with the saying that dinner parties rank next in importance to General Councils! At the Old Palace they were certainly times of happiness and perfect concord and unity. The end of December and the whole of January were practically given up to them. The bishop was given to hospitality. The arrangements of the parties and dinners were a matter of real interest to him; and night after night past Bishops of Lincoln looked from their

The Drawing Room at the Old Palace.

Page 149.

pictures upon the walls over assemblies of happy guests.

Occasionally there were contretemps ; once at Hilton House (the small house in which the bishop lived during the alterations at the Old Palace), when Sir Walter Phillimore (then Chancellor of the Diocese) and Lady Phillimore were staying with him, the bishop had intended to ask ten people to dinner on two successive evenings. On the first evening none of the guests turned up. Next day it was discovered that they had all been asked for the second day. The room, however, could only hold fourteen people, so the unfortunate chaplain was sent round to explain the situa- to some of the best-known guests, and to ask them kindly *not* to come !

The last party in January was always a family party for the household, when the bishop came in and thanked them, and told them how they had helped him all through the year, and that he simply could not have got on without them, and that he wanted them to have a happy and enjoyable evening. On his eightieth birthday they gave him a new hat and gloves, thinking, as they said, "it would be nice and warm for him during the spring

Confirmations." A day or two after, to their great delight, they were all sent for into the study, and found framed and signed copies of the bishop's last photograph as a present for them. The whole household was absolutely devoted to him.

No picture of the bishop would be complete without a word about guests staying in the house. Constantly there were visitors coming and going, for he loved to have friends, young and old, about him ; and he spared no pains to make them feel at home. Even when he was nearly eighty he would sometimes insist on escorting a guest to his bedroom, returning to his own study to finish his letters. But there was one special feature which no one who stayed at the Old Palace can have forgotten—that is what one who knew him intimately has called, "the radiance of his good-byes." "I can see him now standing at the door in his cassock and skull-cap as the carriage drove away, cheering and uplifting you with that wonderful smile on his face." "This world," he would say, "is the place in which to make friendships, but it is in the next world that we shall really enjoy them."

CHAPTER VII

THE BISHOP IN THE VILLAGES AND TOWNS

Si mise a circuir la vigna,
Che tosto imbianca, se il vignaio è reo.
Par. xii. 86–87.

He set himself
To go about the vineyard, that soon turns
To wan and wither'd, if not tended well.
Cary.

CHAPTER VII

THE BISHOP IN THE VILLAGES AND TOWNS

WITHOUT doubt the greatest joy to the bishop, in taking up his work in Lincolnshire, was the thought that he was going back again to the poor.

"I delight to think that I am going to work again amongst the poor," he said.

"To bring home to the people the blessings of the Church" was the predominant aim of his episcopate; and as the diocese is for the most part agricultural, it was the people in the villages to whom his thoughts most naturally turned. He was never so happy as when he was confirming in a country parish. He spoke in such a simple way that all could understand him.

Nor was it only to the young that he appealed. If a baby cried during his sermon, or at a Confirmation, instantly the bishop put himself in the position of the mother. "I don't mind, if you don't. You needn't take it out, you needn't take it out. I don't mind, if you don't." What mother could resist a man who could instinctively interpret her feelings like that ?

In his sermons he always used the simplest words and illustrations. Who can ever forget his Confirmation addresses—their simplicity, yet their depth, their unwearying insistence on the duty of Prayer, Bible-reading, and Holy Communion, the boldness of his illustrations, and his almost reckless repetition till the dullest of his hearers could not fail to apprehend his meaning.

Again and again he would warn the lads and girls against starving their souls. The soul wants feeding, he would insist, no less than the body. "Just as you wouldn't starve your body, so you should not starve your soul. How strange it would be, how foolish, if you were to come in one day and say, 'No, I shan't eat my dinner to-day, or I shan't eat my tea or my supper.' If you were to go on like this, you know what would happen—your body would die. But it's just the same with the soul. Your soul wants food as well as your body. Take a lamb three days old. Take it away from its mother. Give it no milk, nothing to eat; what would happen? You know. It would dwindle and die, and you would have no one else to thank for it!"

Confirmations in the country generally take place in the spring, so that all the children would have seen lambs in the fields, and they would, especially the lads, be caught at once by what the bishop was saying. But his words so far would have been intended primarily for the men and lads, and the bishop would not be content till he had riveted the attention of the girls by an illustration more entirely suited to them; so he would turn their way and speak to them in perhaps graver tones. They would nearly all have little brothers or sisters at home. If the baby were taken away from its mother, if it were not properly fed, they all knew what would happen, they knew who would be to blame. By this time the bishop had thoroughly got the attention of all the candidates and of all the mothers—the baby and the lamb! They stood out clearly in their minds! They had both been dying for want of food! And then he would turn round upon them with his application, and drive home the lesson again and again, repeating and repeating it again and again tenderly, patiently, gently, persistently: "Now it's just the same with your souls, dear children. If you don't say your prayers, if you don't come to Holy Communion, if you don't read your Bibles, *you are starving your souls*; is it any wonder they dwindle and die? Have you anybody to thank but yourself?"

Another year—he generally had one special message each Confirmation tour—he would find manifold ways of putting the candidates on their guard against the danger of being over-shy in religion, of being afraid of letting it be known that they were trying to live good lives for God. *Shyness*, he would say, is the devil's dust—like dust the devil throws in people's eyes to make them afraid of being seen at their prayers or reading their Bibles, or going out in the early morning to Communion. But perhaps one of his boldest and most arresting Confirmation addresses was on the danger of *relapse* and falling away from grace. It is almost impossible to think of any one else daring to use it, or, perhaps, able to put it in such simple and piercing words. It was an account of what might take place at the particular judgement between our Lord and a soul that had fallen away from religion: "My child, how could you? Didn't I call you? Didn't I put you in My Church? Didn't I give you a priest to teach you? Didn't I give you a Prayer Book and a Bible? Didn't I speak to you in your conscience?" And to each question the faltering, hesitating answer of the poor fallen soul. It was the burden of the Confirmation address to more than two hundred candidates in the cathedral, and a vast congregation reaching to the great west doors, where there was hardly even standing room. Some, at any rate, of those who heard his words have never forgotten them, nor are they likely to do.

Sometimes the bishop, when talking of prayer and Bible reading, would stop and say, "But now very likely you would say to me, 'Well, bishop, we have not much time for prayer or reading the Bible; our lives are busy ones.' 'Well,' would come the reply, 'God bless you. I know you haven't much time—at least, not on the weekdays—but there is Sunday! You can get a little time then. God does not expect too much; but you might do it then. And then there are your prayers. Well, God does not want great, long prayers from you. He doesn't want fine words. He just wants you to speak to Him quite naturally; a few words are very often enough. And then there is the Lord's Prayer—you all know the Lord's Prayer—and you can say that.' "

On the question of moral courage he would often speak: "Why don't you read your Bibles? It isn't that you don't believe in God: you do—thank God—believe in Him. It is not always that you have no time; but it is very often that you are ashamed! It is so strange, isn't it? Yet it is true. It is like this—the Bible is something like a letter from GOD. Now, if you had a letter from the King how pleased you would be to be seen reading it! You would like to be seen reading it, and others would come round you and say, 'Have you got a letter from the King?' And you would be proud and pleased. Now the Bible is like a letter from the *King of kings*, so you ought not to be ashamed of reading the Bible! Yet some people are ashamed, and would hide it or sit on it if some one came into the room as they were reading it. This ought not to be. Try and read a verse or two every day from God's Book."

Or he would remind them of how our

Lord used the Bible. "He used the Bible in temptation. What a comfort it is to have that told us, how He used the Bible to ward off temptation! We might have thought that if the devil is so audacious as to tempt the Saviour, the angels would have brushed him away, and that it would never be spoken about. No; the Saviour is too loving for that; He would let the devil come and try his very worst at Him, and He would wish it written down in the Gospels that the devil did do it. Why? To give you comfort, dear children. If the devil tempts you to do wrong, don't be out of heart all in a hurry; don't think because he tempts you, 'Ah! I'm done for!' The devil went up to the Saviour with great impudence, and told lies in His face; and notice how the Saviour beat him off. He quoted back to him a text out of the Bible. You remember that when the devil went to the Saviour he wanted Him to turn the stones into bread. But the Saviour said very quietly, 'No, I won't do it; it is written, "Man shall not live by bread alone."' He brushed him off by quoting bits out of the Bible, which (I think we may say with reverence) most likely the Saviour had stored up in His mind when He was younger, just as you may remember bits out of the Catechism, or things you have learnt. He used the Bible against the tempter; so when the devil comes to you, think of some text in the Bible, lift up your heart and say, 'Show Thou me the way that I should walk in, for I lift up my soul unto Thee.' 'Speak, Lord, for Thy servant heareth,' 'Lord, save me.' When the temptation comes, don't be frightened, but remember how the Saviour used the Bible to drive the devil away. Then when He was crucified on the Cross He again used the words of the Bible—'My God, My God, why hast Thou forsaken Me?' 'Into Thy hands I commend My spirit'; and He adds a little word, you remember—'*Father*,' showing you the way to use the Bible in order to make it your own." [1]

Another very characteristic feature of the bishop's Confirmation addresses is the extreme simplicity with which he speaks of "the Saviour's" life. "Think," he says, "If the Saviour was not above being born in a stable, and placed in a manger, He won't be above coming to me, though my house may be very

[1] *Sermons and Addresses* (Longmans), p. 195.

simple and my room very poor." Again, to one who is supposed to say, "I shall never be in a very rich way," he replies, "Well, was the Saviour? Did the Saviour ever make a fortune? Was He ever in a way of business? Yes, He was . . . the Saviour was pleased to work in a shop, but where? Not in a big town, but just in a little village—Nazareth, a little out-of-the-way country place, and one that people did not think much of—indeed, they despised it; and there, in a little shop (He was never in a big way of business) He worked as a carpenter day after day, quite quietly, till He was thirty years of age, and within three years of His death. That is a great comfort to us. If you have to work in a little shop, in a little family, in a little way; if you feel you will never make a big fortune, it is very nice and comfortable to think, 'Nor did the Saviour, and therefore He will be with me, and I may be with Him. He did work, but He was never in a big way of business, was never made anything of in this world.' Now I say it should be a great comfort to you, and should prevent you losing your self-respect because there may be other people who are richer than you. It is the heart God looks at; it is the life He values, not the person, nor the money." [1]

One great mark of his work in the country parishes, and indeed throughout the diocese, was his thoroughness. He would never scamp his visits. He would never, if he could help it, leave a parish hurriedly after the service; he would always wait and see any one who wished to see him. He would stay to luncheon, or tea, or dinner, or supper (if he could), and was unwearied in his talks to Church-workers or Churchwardens, to neighbours asked to meet him—to anybody, in fact, who wanted to have a word with the bishop. In this way he got to know not only the clergy, but the laity as well. It was known that he was thoroughly *accessible*—(the word that Bishop Wilberforce once said he would like to see written over every parsonage door), and that he was ready to talk to and help any one who liked to come and see him; and who ever saw him bored? The immense expenditure of force which this entailed would have been impossible to him in his early days; but in later life he seemed to gather strength as the years went on, and he was rarely over-tired, even so, always perfectly

[1] *Sermons and Addresses*, pp. 193, 194.

The Bishop taking part in a Procession (about 1906).

Page 163.

fresh again after a night's rest. And if any one remarked next morning on his recovery from over-fatigue he would say, "Yes! my dear mother always used to say I responded to treatment."

In towns and villages alike, after the first few months of his episcopate, he used habitually to wear his cope and mitre; he was, in fact, the first diocesan bishop to revive the use of the mitre in England[1]—but never without the full concurrence of the incumbent of the parish in which he was officiating. There were, however, very few incumbents who did not welcome the revival of these ancient insignia of a bishop's office.

With regard to other matters of ceremonial, he had worn the chasuble and the other Eucharistic vestments for many years as a priest, and he continued to do so in his private chapel when he became a bishop, and he used wafer-bread; but this made no difficulty in the diocese; he would always wear the vestments in any church where it was the custom to do so. It must not be supposed, however, that the bishop cared about externals

[1] The first occasion of his wearing the mitre in his cathedral was at the Advent Ordination, 1885.

for their own sake. He neither knew nor cared anything about the *minutiae* of ritual. His feeling was that the revival of Catholic ceremonial was a great witness to the continuity of the Church which it would be misleading and shortsighted not to make use of. It must be allowed that the true significance of the cope and mitre was not always duly appreciated by all the onlookers.

One God-fearing old lady at Lincoln gave it as her opinion that the bishop was a "dear old gentleman, but a wee bit too gay for a Gospel minister!"

Wherever he went in the diocese he used to take his pastoral-staff. In doing this he simply followed the example of his great predecessor. The people all over the diocese knew that the one thing he really cared for was to bring men, women, and children nearer to God, and to make their lives brighter and happier in the consciousness of the love of God and of the Communion of Saints. His great aim was, as he used to say, to get the "piety of the people" more and more on to Church lines, so that they might learn to value and to frequent the Sacraments increasingly, and by their diligent use of them to become more "Christ-like Christians."

The bishop's tender ministrations to prisoners condemned to death must not be overlooked. Two or three times, at least, he undertook this duty; and then one may be quite sure that all his pastoral love for souls was poured out in one concentrated stream on the object of his pity and his prayers. On the first occasion his undertaking this duty was owing to the fact that the chaplain at the gaol was inexperienced, and either asked the bishop to help him or consulted the bishop in his difficulty. The case thus passed into the bishop's hands, and for a week or two he went every day to the prison on his return from his Confirmation work. The present writer remembers the bishop telling him that he had been teaching the poor man (who was entirely ignorant of the Christian religion) about the Prodigal Son. In the end, he made his confession and received the Holy Communion; and the bishop was with him till he went to the scaffold.

"You have seen, I dare say," he wrote to one of his chaplains some years after, "that we are in trouble here again—a poor, dear

Grimsby fisherman; it will all be over in a fortnight to-morrow. Will you please remember him, H—— R——, and ask that he may be forgiven and accepted; and for me, that my sins may not hinder my helping him. We have every hope for him; he is really most beautiful. I am just back from the gaol, so my hand shakes, but not for him; it is a great privilege, if we are only equal to it. But you will remember poor Richard [the first criminal of this kind to whom he had ministered], and understand that I cannot help asking God to hear his prayer for me now, if it be His will. I think it is, and it seems so easy."[1]

There is little to be said about Bishop King's work in the towns of the diocese which has not already been said in regard to the villages. Grimsby and Lincoln are the only two large towns, and it was a constant source of anxiety to the bishop how to keep pace in the matter of church-building and spiritual provision with the growth of the population, and how to overtake the arrears in such matters which even the energy and foresight of Bishop Wordsworth had not been able to prevent.

[1] *Spiritual Letters*, p. 169.

The Rev. A. W. Ballachey, writes :—

"In Grimsby especially the problem was acute. Very soon after Dr. King became bishop he showed his real interest in the matter by offering a large and generous donation towards building an iron church for a large and growing district. The priest-in-charge of the district asked the bishop if he would allow his gift to be used to build a school or hall that could be used for Services and other purposes until a permanent church should be built.

"The bishop replied :—

"'The question is really a part of a very large one. I think there is a danger of turning our churches into club-rooms and concert-rooms, and trusting to such agencies instead of the real Gospel Message. Five years or so of solid spiritual work would be to my mind, more valuable for the future of the Church than the more popular kind of work which is increasingly prevailing in the present time. I am not against the use of these secondary agencies, but I think there is a danger of their becoming primary.' And so the iron church was built."

In the year 1901 the bishop issued a Commission to inquire into the spiritual needs of Grimsby and the neighbourhood; and a Grimsby Church Extension Fund was set up to carry out the suggestions of the Commission. The bishop was a most generous supporter of the fund, and in his visitation charge of 1904 made an appeal to the whole diocese to help the work.

"It is the greatest responsibility in our diocese," he writes. "There are over 80,000 souls in Grimsby and only church accommodation for 6,000. I hope every parish in the diocese will try to realize that the diocese is the true ecclesiastical unit, and not the parish, and send some contribution to our Grimsby Church Extension Fund."

Support for the bishop's scheme came from practically all parts of the country. On the occasion of his eightieth birthday a sum of £2,000 was presented to him by friends in the diocese; this sum was allocated to the Building Fund of St. Luke's, Grimsby—the beautiful church which has since been built as a memorial to the bishop. The relations existing between the bishop and his clergy in Grimsby were of the most intimate and affectionate character, and whenever he came to

Grimsby he was always sure of the warmest welcome.

In his acknowledgement of the cheque, the bishop wrote :—

"I can assure you that this expression of your kindness has been a very great comfort to me, and it will, I hope, encourage me to persevere and try to do better during the time that I may yet be spared to live and work amongst you. I am specially pleased to hear that the great sum includes many small gifts. The real comfort of a gift is the love that it represents. The birthday gifts of children to their parents are precious according to the love which the parents have for their children, and the love of the children represented by their gifts.

"So it is, my dear children, with a father in God. But your great gift means something more than kindly feeling towards myself. You have given a real help to the extension of God's Holy Church in Grimsby. For this only God Himself can duly bless you. I pray to God to remember you concerning this, and to reward you according to His perfect wisdom and love."

Several large legacies from Grimsby people

were bequeathed to the fund, and the sum originally suggested was eventually raised, and the proposed additions and alterations in the ecclesiastical parishes of Grimsby duly carried out.

The bishop's intense interest in the work may be considered as the primary cause of the success; all were glad to give and work on behalf of a movement which he had so deeply at heart. This great achievement will always remain as a monument to his lengthened and wise episcopate, and to the affection held for him by all, whether clergy or laymen, in the diocese.

In regard to Lincoln itself, it was the bishop's great delight to associate himself with any good work which was being carried on in the different parishes. He won the affection of all classes; but perhaps it was the railway men for whom he felt a special affection. He recognized how much he owed them as he was continually travelling over the diocese; he was always ready to say a few words at the meetings of the Church Railway Guild.

On September 19, 1909, he spoke what were probably his last words to the members of this guild. His subject was the Great

Supper, and the special point which he was emphasizing was our Lord's *gentleness*, but the words seem, looking back on them, to be prophetic; he saw clearly that the danger in a materialistic age was that people, while becoming outwardly respectable and well behaved, should ignore the claims of religion, and neglect their duty to God. "He never exaggerates, never wishes to make people out worse than they are. He tries to make the best of people, and when He must point out their faults to warn them, He does it with a gentleness that no one could deny, or say that He has spoken too hardly or not shown that gentleness is the absolute and awful truth. The text is an example of what I mean; they are quiet, gentle words, but they describe the behaviour of those who will be shut out of the kingdom of heaven,

"'They all with one consent began to make excuse.'

"Now who were the people, and what had they done? Nothing that we should call very bad, they are not charged with stealing or murder or drunkenness or dishonesty or blasphemy; all that is said about them is that 'they made excuse.' The wrong was that they put worldly interests and pleasures in the place of their duty to God. They made light of God's call to heavenly things; they made excuses that they could not attend to the duties of religion. Now, dear friends, are not these gentle words of our Blessed Lord just the very warning that we want at the present time?

"The danger to religion at the present day is '*Indifference*.' It is exactly what our Lord in His parable has expressed in His gentle words: 'They made light of it, and begged to be excused.' Now it is for this reason that I am so thankful to come again to speak to you in connection with the Railway Guild. The railway men, as I have said, are a fine body of honest, sober men, and a guild is exactly what we want to help us to keep up the rule of our religious duties, and bring others to do the same. By so doing you will be helping in the very way in which Christianity wants help in the present day of material and intellectual progress. Christianity wants to be kept religious."

The bishop's relations with the Mayor and Corporation of Lincoln were always most happy. He let no difference of religious opinion interfere with his intercourse with any of them. Early in his episcopate, as soon as he was really established at the Old Palace, he asked the Mayor and Corporation to dinner soon after Christmas, and this dinner became an annual institution, and contributed in no small measure to help those who held office in the city to know the bishop, while he took pains to interest himself in any scheme which might be set on foot for the benefit of the citizens of Lincoln. In this way the members of the Corporation soon came to realize that they had in the bishop a friend who was ready to help on any work for the social wellbeing of the community.

All enjoyed the bishop's open-handed hospitality, but it was the bishop himself and his friendly intercourse with every one that they really appreciated.

At Lincoln there are large engineering and agricultural works, and the foundrymen were a constant source of interest to the bishop; and they quite certainly had a place in his prayers, as he told some of them when he was living at Hilton House, and when he could hear them passing under his window every morning. And besides the workmen there are apt to be a considerable number of apprentices in the works, many of them sons of the clergy or of professional men. The bishop used to make a point of seeing any of these young men whom he might get to know through letters of introduction, or in any other way. His chief plan was to ask them up one at a time to luncheon on Sunday, and to get a talk with them afterwards.

But even when in Lincoln his thoughts often wandered off to the villages on the wold or in the fens. How he used to delight to go out on market-day and watch the carriers' carts starting out from the Bailgate. "Do look at that box, dear friend," he would say. "Think of the expectation that it is exciting in some village. How they will be watching for it! Perhaps it is something for the children; market-day, you know, is a day of expectation in the country villages. Some of the family come in to Lincoln and 'shop' for the others."

From first to last he was a pastoral bishop, with the true heart of a pastor, sharing in the joys of his people no less than in their sorrows. His diocese was to him one big parish, which it was his privilege and joy to serve.

"He was content to go up and down every corner of the diocese, and to take a whole day, on hopeless side-lines, reaching some far village in the wolds, and laying his hands on a half-dozen beloved ploughboys. . . .

"He delighted in the far-away look to be caught in the eyes of the shepherds on the wolds, always steadying their faces to scrutinize something seen approaching from out of the distance. 'Be yon a beast, or be yon a man?' That is the sort of gaze with which they greeted you. He loved one of them who had slowly learned that the candles on the altar were lighted in broad daylight because they had no utilitarian purpose. They were not there to give light, but to bear witness. 'Eh! then yours is a yon-side religion, I see, sir.' It appeals, he meant, to something beyond this world. The porters loved him, the villagers loved him, the town loved him. Twice I went down to Lincoln Fair with him, all among the coco-nuts and the gingerbread and the fat woman. It was a delicious experience to note the affection that followed him about. He drew out love as the sun draws fragrance from the flowers. He moved in an atmosphere of love." [1]

[1] H. S. Holland, in *A Bundle of Memories.*

THE LINCOLN JUDGEMENT

He would have been thankful to have been left to carry on his work at Lincoln with steady courage and zeal; but it was so ordered that he should be thrust into a very unwelcome prominence by the ritual case, which eventuated in what is known as the Lincoln Judgement.

Owing mainly to influences outside the diocese, directed by a powerful organization, evidence was taken against the bishop when he was celebrating the Holy Eucharist in the cathedral and when he was consecrating the additions to the Church of St. Peter-at-Gowts, Lincoln, in December of the year 1887.

The points on which the bishop was attacked were the eastward position during the Prayer of Consecration, lighted candles on the altar, the mixture of water with wine in the chalice, the *Agnus Dei* after the Consecration, the sign of the Cross at the Absolution and Blessing, and the ablution of the sacred vessels.

Formal complaint was made to the Archbishop of Canterbury (Dr. Benson), who decided to try the case in his own court, with five episcopal assessors. The court sat in

February, 1890, and judgement was given in the autumn of the same year. It forbade the ceremonial mixture of the chalice and the use of the sign of the Cross at the Absolution and Benediction, and required that the manual acts should be visible to the people. On all other points it was in the bishop's favour. He wrote to the archdeacons and rural deans of the diocese, saying that he was "most thankful to be able conscientiously to comply with the archbishop's judgement," and drawing their attention to certain points which appeared "to demand especial thankfulness":—

"1. That the Judgement is based on independent inquiry, and that it recognizes the continuity of the English Church.

"2. That the primitive, and all but universal, custom of administering a Mixed Cup in the Holy Eucharist has been preserved.

"3. That the remaining Elements may be reverently consumed by the cleansing of the vessels immediately after the close of the Service.

"4. That it is allowable by the use of two Lights, and of singing, during the Celebration of the Holy Communion to assist the devotion of our people."

No doubt the strain of the whole affair told upon his health and strength—at least for a time. He hated being dragged so much into public notice. He would immeasurably have preferred to be left in peace to carry on his work in the diocese ; but he never complained ; and, when the case was settled, and he had recovered from his illness, he took up the threads of his work again with unabated vigour and delight.

CHAPTER VIII

THE BISHOP AND HIS CLERGY

Ecco chi crescera li nostri amori !

Par. v. 105.

Lo, one who will increase our love !

CHAPTER VIII

THE BISHOP AND HIS CLERGY

"ECCO chi crescera li nostri amori!"—"Lo, one who will increase our love!" They are the words with which Dante was welcomed by the spirits who were manifested in one of the spheres of Paradise. There could be no higher standard for a bishop in his relations with his clergy. They are called to special "loves"—the love of God, the love of the Church, the love of devotion, the love of holiness, the love of souls. The bishop and leader they need is one who, in Dante's words, might help to increase their love.

Let us try to see how Bishop King endeavoured to fulfil this high responsibility.

Here is a noble passage in which he set forth very early in his episcopate the standard of clerical life and work:—

"If we are to undertake a spiritual charge—the cure of souls—we must be spiritual men, men of sincere, unaffected, inward piety, men of prayer—men, that is, who know the privileges of having access to the Father in the power of the Spirit, through the mediation of the Son. . . . We must know what prayer and worship mean ourselves before we can hope to direct and lead the worship of the people.

"We need men who have thought out, as far as they can, their own relation to God, and who have realized the strength of the complex proof on which it depends; men who have walked in the threefold light of their own faculties, of revelation, and of the Church; and have seen how the three agree and lead back to one.

"We need men who have disciplined their reason by endeavouring to discern and speak the exact truth, without fear of the reproof of man, and without the desire of his praise.

"We need men who have endeavoured to keep a conscience void of offence, not only in the sight of men, but of God; men who can, like Bishop Andrewes, pray God to 'crucify the occasions of their sins'; men who have striven to cleanse themselves from all filthiness, not only of the flesh, but of the spirit; men who exercise 'themselves unto godliness, perfecting holiness in the fear of the Lord.'

"We need men whose eyes have been opened by the power of the Holy Ghost, so that they can 'say that Jesus is the Lord'; who can see 'all power given unto Him in heaven and earth to be the Head of the Church, which is His Body.'

"We need men who are rooted and grounded in and constrained by love; men who will be patient with sinners and those who are ignorant and careless and 'out of the way'; men who will wait and watch for single souls, as the Saviour did for the woman of Samaria at the well, though she was a woman of a false theology and a broken character; men who will love and not grow cold, but who, having loved, like Jesus, will 'love to the end'; men who know the Church to be a true Society, and, as such, to possess all those natural assistances which the wisest of the heathen of old sought to secure for the individual by his relation to the State; men who see the Church to be divine in her origin, in her organization, and in her powers—a Divine Society of which Christ is the living animating Head; men who see that the ordinances of the Church are not barriers between the soul and its God, but the appointed means by which the soul shall return to God, by the mediation of the one Mediator, Christ—both God and Man; men who desire to draw all men within the fold of the visible Church of Christ, because there they will find their true relation to God and to their fellow-men. In her they are reconciled back to God and reunited to man in the Communion of Saints, and in her receive new powers that this two-fold communion may endure for ever and ever." [1]

It is a great ideal of priestly life. It might well serve as matter for thought and self-examination and inspiration on Ember Days, or in seasons of quiet devotion. It was preached in a sermon to a great gathering of clergy in the cathedral at the first Festival of the *Scholae Cancellarii* [2] in 1888. It is a message St. Hugh might well have desired to be given to his sons. Its teachings formed the groundwork of the addresses given by the bishop at many retreats and quiet days for the clergy of the diocese.

One of these stands out above others, a

[1] *The Love and Wisdom of God*, pp. 272 sq.

[2] The theological school of the diocese founded by St. Hugh, and re-established by Bishop Wordsworth.

Diocesan Retreat held in the cathedral in September, 1892, the first of a long series of such retreats or spiritual conferences. The bishop was desirous of gathering his clergy together once every year for a season of thought and devotion in the cathedral. It was not exactly in the technical sense of the term a Retreat, but it took a form well suited for the clergy of the diocese, most of whom were in charge of country parishes, and whose lives were passed in much loneliness and isolation. The Retreats were three days' devotions, with special Eucharists and spiritual conferences delivered by some of the greatest masters of spiritual life in the English Church. It was a wonderful refreshment and inspiration to be brought, year by year, under the influence of great teachers who, but for these conferences, would have been known by little more than their names and their writings to most of the clergy of the diocese.

The bishop himself conducted the first of these gatherings; and one who was present has contributed the following brief and vivid account of his memories and impressions:—

"We had, of course, often seen the bishop and heard him preach on special occasions.

Now we seemed really to know him for the first time, to feel his whole heart and soul laid open to his clergy. It is impossible adequately to summarize or describe the addresses. They were searching and uplifting. We felt 'the spiritual life around the earthly life.' There was boldness of illustration, swift description, the light touch that photographed a character or an experience never to be forgotten, new and unexpected comments on familiar passages or scenes in Holy Scripture. There were flashes of humour, and then piercing appeals that drew swift, hot tears. There was a fearless confidence that everything would go home, everything be understood. He was the theologian setting forth the deepest teachings of the Faith; the master of ethics playing with Aristotle and the anti-pelagian treatises of St. Augustine, as we might have done with the multiplication-table; the spiritual guide bringing it all into relation with every sphere of our life and duty. And it was all done with such ease and naturalness: it seemed absolutely inevitable.

"What renewal of hopes! What possibilities were before us. We could be something of all that. It was so deep and yet so simple.

We could be penitent and forgiven and start again. We had seen it all. We had a bishop, a friend, a father who knew and understood."

With such an ideal of clerical life it will be clear that Bishop King would take immense pains in the arrangement of Ordinations and the influences brought to bear upon ordinands at that season.

A short reference to the Retreat immediately preceding the Ordination must suffice for the purpose of this chapter. Three days of special preparation were arranged ; and the addresses and devotions were entrusted to some priest experienced in pastoral work. There were daily Eucharists and rules of discipline and silence. The bishop always gave the last address on the night before the Ordination. He felt an almost overwhelming sense of responsibility, and he had an extraordinary realization of the gifts of ministerial grace. It was often thought that he deliberately held in reserve the personal influence which he might have been expected to use to the full at such a time. His chaplains were sometimes almost disappointed. But he probably knew exactly what he was doing. He wanted the men to be brought into absolutely direct fellowship with God. He wanted their experience to rest not on the wisdom of man but on the power of God. He spoke deep and searching words about the necessity of a realized vocation, the need of a cleansed and forgiven soul, the quiet restfulness in which he trusted they were waiting for the great gift that was coming to them. And often, as he brought into his final words some message from Dante—"the great companion," as he called him—he seemed to have something of Dante's greatness of love, of his serious and even austere outlook on life, of his almost infinite hope. But the ordinands were always left in the last silence with God and their own souls face to face, no human influence thrust in between.

It was the bishop's custom to hold triennial visitations. The preparation of the address was always a matter of most serious concern to him. The primary charge, which has already been fully referred to, was a pronouncement to the diocese, the forecast of work he believed he was sent to undertake. In later charges the bishop set forth somewhat fully the doctrines of Holy Communion, Absolution, the Unity of the Church, and Holy Marriage. His method of exposition does not easily lend itself to quotation. He set forth his teaching in the statements of theologians of "high position and allowed orthodoxy" in the Church of England rather than in language of his own. People often wished that he had been more ready to put his doctrinal message in his own words. But the charges are of very real value, and the method of exposition is significant of his intense loyalty to the Church in which he held office as a bishop and teacher of the Faith.

All the addresses make special and detailed reference to the work of the diocese, and abound in wise and loving suggestions as to methods of pastoral work. Perhaps the third triennial charge is one of the most characteristic. It was delivered shortly after the Clergy Retreat in the cathedral, conducted by the bishop, in September, 1892. It deals with the danger of indifference, and urges ministerial zeal as its great antidote. The following quotations well represent the bishop's thoughts on the subject; and the beauty and simplicity, as well as the directness and sincerity, of his appeal:—

"The opposite of indifference is obviously zeal. How, then, can we promote more zeal

—religious zeal—amongst our people? The answer I wish to offer to you, my brethren, and to myself with you, is this:—By being more zealous in our calling ourselves. Is not the indifference of the laity the result, in part, of the indifference of the clergy? Thank God! I know what improvement there has been; how many zealous clergymen, and clergymen's families, there are amongst us now. But still, has there not been in the past enough indifference amongst ourselves to the special duties of our sacred calling to account for a part, at least, of the indifference amongst our people? Have not their highest spiritual desires and aspirations often been *disappointed*, so far as we are concerned? They have expected us to be more holy, more helpful in spiritual things than they have found us. They have looked for grapes, and have found only wild grapes. They have hoped for the fruit of the Spirit—love, joy, peace; and they have seen in us little more than the results of natural religion—prudence, justice, fortitude, and temperance! . . . Do not misunderstand me, dear brothers. No one is more fearful than myself of having wasted time in lingering on the lower level of natural religion instead of ascending the Mount of Transfiguration with the Saviour, in the power of the Spirit. I grieve to feel myself but a child in reading the Gospels and Epistles when old age is closing upon me. But it is because I am conscious of this in myself that I feel constrained to say this to you. Let us try to live more as a reader of the Gospels and Epistles would expect to find us living."

The bishop then goes on to speak in some detail of "Frequency of Communion" :—

"We need it, do we not, dear brethren, for ourselves? What is the great difficulty which we labour under in our small and scattered parishes? Is it not isolation, the sense of loneliness, and that depression and loss of heart which arises from isolation and the sense of loneliness? And where shall we find a better remedy for all this than in the constant renewing of our Communion with our Divine Lord, in the way which He has Himself provided for us? Under the old law the priest was bound to rekindle the fire upon the altar, and to trim the lamps of the sanctuary every day. And so we need to rekindle the fire of our love and zeal, by putting ourselves in the closest relation we can with the Source of zeal and love, even with Him of whom it is written, 'The zeal of Thine House hath eaten me up.' Let us do this at least at the beginning of each week, through the means which He has Himself appointed. He is 'the Light of the world,' and we are to shine as 'lights in the world' by His light reflected in us. We must therefore put ourselves in His presence, and endeavour to preserve unbroken through the week the Communion into which we are thus taken.

"We need this frequency of Communion for our own souls, and for our ministerial efficiency. And do we not need it for our people? Is not one of the things which most grieves and depresses us in them the low view they take of the sinfulness of sin? They are content to regard sin, not as it appears in the eyes of God, but according to the traditional standard of their own village, or according to the standard which they pick up from the newspapers, or from the current tone of public opinion. They use all kinds of minimizing phrases in speaking of it. Now where, my brethren, shall we learn what God thinks of sin, but at the Cross of Calvary, where we see the Son of God dying for the sins of the world? And might it not be one effect of the constant weekly celebration of the Holy Communion if our people knew that week by week we were pleading that one 'full, perfect, and sufficient Sacrifice' for the remission of sins, that they might learn to look on sin more in the light in which God sees it, and no longer rest satisfied with the low standard of morality which we have so often to deplore?

"And we need it for the faithful few. Scattered about, even in our smallest parishes, one here and one there, are those whose hearts God has touched, who only want to be drawn out and sustained in those aspirations which we cannot see, and which we are not worthy to know, but which we may by our divinely-given ministry assist.

"Lastly we need this frequent Celebration for the sake of the whole Church; for God answers prayer beyond all that we ask or think, and for the praise and glory of the Lord, whose death we thus show forth until He come."

Later, in the same charge, the bishop urges a fuller obedience to the Church's directions as to the regular and public use of the Daily Offices:—

"I desire to ask all to consider this matter

afresh in the light of the present indifference, and to see whether more might not be done in this direction which our Church has so plainly pointed out for us. The difficulties, I know, are most real and great, especially in country parishes. In some cases, I am ready to allow, they are insuperable . . . but still I do desire that, wherever it may be, the bell should ring out, at least once a day, to give notice of a service in church. I cannot but hope that, if every day the bell were to sound, it might do something to dispel the indifference which is so much around us.

"There may from time to time be some one lying upon the bed of death, some one whom we have been unable to reach by our sermons or admonitions, some one who has not yet turned to God; and the sound of the bell from the House of God borne in upon the ear may, by God's grace, strike the soul with that wondrous power which belongs to sacred music; and the wanderer, even in that last hour, may think of God, and turn again and pray and be forgiven.

"Or there may be others not so near the end as this, but still confined to the house by age or sickness, and liable to that despondency and depression which continued weakness and inability to take part in the business of life so often bring; and the sound of the bell may lead their thoughts upward, and recall them to a sense of what this life really is—the school, nay, rather the infant school, for the true life beyond.

"Then there are those who are at their work, and cannot come, whom we would not have to come. But do we not desire that, while they are at work they should feel that they are doing God's will—that while they are walking in the furrow, following the plough, they may still be walking in the spirit? And will not the sound of the Church bell bring to their minds the thought of God and of the world to come?

"So again with others who might come from time to time. There are two calendars which might bring people to church on certain days. There is the Church Calendar, with its saints' days and other holy days; and there is a Domestic Calendar, which is observed in almost every house, indeed, almost by every single person. A man would say to himself, 'To-morrow is my birthday, and I should like to go to church to thank God for my life; and to pray Him to forgive the way I have wasted my time, and to give me strength to use what may be left to better purpose.' Or, 'To-morrow is my wedding day, and I should like to thank God for the blessings He then bestowed upon me, blessings more than I had any idea of at the time.' Or, 'To-morrow is the day God gave us our first child; or the day He took that child to Himself; and ever since it has been to me as a guiding-star in heaven.' So there would often be somebody in some corner of the church, for reasons of which we might know nothing; but God would know, and God would hear them." [1]

The bishop knew and loved his clergy. He understood their difficulties; he knew that sometimes the standard might seem too high, too impossible. He had always words of encouragement:—

"Perhaps you have found it harder than you thought; perhaps you are surprised at the indifference and the ignorance which still prevails

[1] A correspondent writes: "In four or five huge gatherings of the clergy in Lincoln the bishop always drove home the intense reality of the Daily Offices, and implored for *no omission* of the 'State Prayers.' 'Never was there an age when King and Queen more needed our prayers than now. O my brothers, don't rob King, Queen, and country of your help.'"

with regard to the Church amongst your people; perhaps, as priests, when visiting the sick you have felt unable to use the Office which your Church has provided for her children; perhaps you are disappointed with your brethren of the clergy around you; perhaps you are surprised and disappointed with yourselves. Do not be disheartened; these, and such as these, are the trials by which the priests of the Church of England are being tried; they often are not understood, not wanted, not cared for; isolated, lonely, unnoticed, unknown by the world; and all this has to be borne too often now in poverty which cannot be expressed, and it may be in actual sickness, or under the intimidation of declining health. So are many priests left now, but it shall not be for nothing. It is all under the Saviour's eye. He is watching, He is working; it is His Father's business that He is about, making the English priesthood *holy*; not simply intelligent, not simply moral, but *holy*. The Saviour is watching, and the people are watching too. Whatever they may be themselves, they expect that if the Church is holy the ministry will be holy too—a city set on a hill cannot be hid." [1]

[1] *Love and Wisdom*, p. 275.

Encouragement is for most people one of the greatest needs in life. It is so especially with many of the clergy. There are those who have found their way almost fully and completely to the Source of all Comfort, and who go with bright, glad hearts through any trouble or difficulty. But there are others. It is not easy to know exactly when consolation and comfort is in danger of weakening rather than of strengthening and quickening into new life. Bishop King knew the peril well enough, but he seems never to have feared it, always to have been ready to risk it. He knew, on occasion, how to speak sharp, stern words of warning, and the fact that they were spoken so seldom gave them an added force. In one of his charges he felt driven to say: "There are some parishes where I cannot but fear there has been grave and culpable neglect; parishes from which there have been either no candidates at all, or so few as to make it impossible for me to believe that due attention has been given to this most important part of your duties." The words almost flame out with the wrath of gentleness in the midst of a charge full of love and gratitude and humility about his own shortcomings. But it was nearly always through love and gentleness that he put new heart and courage into people. And the strange thing was that he did not set himself to do it. We felt he knew, he understood, he saw the difficulties just as much as we did; but he spoke as if we were doing what we wished to do when we were at our best. He seemed to be winning encouragement for himself out of our difficulties, and we went away with newness of hope and strength. It was really something of his own life we had seen, and it passed into our lives. It was the way of the Gospel of Christ, not of the Old Law.

CHAPTER IX

FRIENDSHIP AND INFLUENCE

Il bene, in quanto ben, come s' intende,
Così accende amore, e tanto maggio,
Quanto più di bontate in sè comprende.
Par. xxvi. 28–30.

Good, inasmuch as we perceive the good,
Kindles our love ; and in degree the more,
As it comprises more of goodness in it.
Cary.

CHAPTER IX

FRIENDSHIP AND INFLUENCE

ENOUGH has been said already to show what a genius Bishop King had for making friends with *all* with whom he came in contact. The influence of such a man in such a position was of course very great.

Immediately after his death Canon Crowfoot wrote the following in the *Diocesan Magazine* :[1] "He was universally beloved, more and more as years went on, with a stronger and deeper love throughout the length and breadth of his diocese. He threw his spell over Lincoln at once. 'A nice, comfortable sort of gentleman,' was the verdict of an old Lincolnshire waiter, after a large luncheon in very early days. It was a homely phrase, but it hit the mark. Wherever the bishop went the charm of his presence brought sunshine and happiness ; it made all about him feel at their ease, and then acted as a magnet for drawing

[1] April, 1910.

out all that was good in them. 'If we can get the bishop all will go well' became a proverb in the diocese. 'I wish to be good for quite a long time after I have been with the bishop. The very sight of his face makes me feel that wish,' said a young officer. And that was the experience of very many of all classes, high and low. 'You made me the happiest woman in the world (referring to the bishop having officiated at her wedding). I will not refuse to do anything you ask me to do,' said a great and gracious lady when asked by the bishop to open a bazaar. 'I have conducted this Retreat because the bishop asked me to do it,' said a bishop when a vote of thanks was proposed. 'If the bishop asked me to do the most impossible thing, I should try.' His sympathy created faith and hope in all who would open their hearts to receive it. The Archbishop (Benson) of Canterbury was attracted by what he called his 'heavenly-mindedness.' The beautiful face was in him the index of a beautiful soul. He had indeed grown up 'like a gentleman, with nothing between him and heaven.' His unfailing courtesy, with its notes of distinction and high breeding, was the gift of his birth and his home. But, as he could not entertain an unkind thought, he could not say an unkind word; and, as he treated all, whatever their rank, whether high or low, as if they were what they ought to be, an influence of irresistible charm flowed from him. The sympathy behind that deep blue eye revealed to him at a glance what to say, and how to say it. His gifts of utterance were unique; and they were gifts—but they were his own; just as the flies with which he caught trout as a boy were all of his own making and ever irresistibly attractive, so was it when he became a fisher of men. His gifts of speech placed at his disposal powers of expression which gave even to quite familiar truths, as they fell from his lips, an added grace and life which they had never seemed before to have. His way of putting words together—whether in ordinary conversation or in a set speech, or in sermons, or in addresses when he was conducting a Retreat—was all of his own making, and was irresistibly attractive."

"My first acquaintance with Bishop King," writes the Earl of Yarborough, "was in July, 1885, shortly after he came into the diocese.

"The occasion was the county agricultural show at Grimsby, for which he came as my guest to Brocklesby.

"At the luncheon he responded, of course, for the toast of the 'Bishop and Clergy': it was the first occasion many of us had met him, and I well remember the deep impression he made on his hearers. Among my guests was my brother-in-law, Francis Astley-Corbett, then a subaltern in the Scots Guards, who had fought in the Egyptian campaign of 1884, and came home very ill with enteric fever contracted at Suakim. On the platform, waiting for the train to convey us all into Grimsby, my huntsman, Will Dale, greeted the young officer very cordially, and, shaking him by the hand, said, 'Glad to see you back, sir.' The bishop made that greeting a text for his speech, delighted as he always was to bring in some homely reference on which to found his lessons. His sympathy and kindly remarks brought tears to some of those who heard him.

"The bishop was then fifty-six, and perhaps looked more than his years owing to his bowed head which, as Mr. Russell has shown in his work, was merely a physical habit, and implied no diminution of general strength. I was only a young man of twenty-six, but so far from experiencing any alarm in talking to so distinguished an ecclesiastic, and one so much older than myself, I felt it a delight and a privilege to be in conversation with him. In fact, I fell under the spell of his charm, and felt instinctively the love he possessed for the association of younger men.

"He visited us on a good many occasions during his episcopate, chiefly when called into the neighbourhood for Confirmations, and Lady Yarborough and I always anticipated these visits with pleasure. He was always so broad-minded in his interests and his conversation. Here at Brocklesby, during the winter months, we were a good deal absorbed in the pleasures of fox-hunting, which was our chief relaxation, and it might be thought there was not much in common between a learned prelate and the young men and women he met in our house; but he always showed a warm interest in the sport, and would be glad to talk about it and the influence for good fellowship it engendered. He would invariably, in those days, stroll up to the kennels and talk over hunting matters with my huntsman, Will Dale, and inquire tenderly after his wife, who was crippled with rheumatic fever. I have always understood that as a young man at Oxford he was an expert horseman; and, though his modest nature never gave a hint of this, his interest in riding never appeared to fail.

"He was once preaching at a Confirmation in Limber church soon after Will Dale had broken his leg through his horse falling over wire placed in a fence. The bishop brought the incident happily into his address in order to impress his hearers that it is not only the great dangers and temptations which must be guarded against, but that the smaller faults, like the hidden wire which we fail to notice, are apt to trip us up in life.

"The bishop and I some twenty years ago were guests of Mr. E. G. Pretyman at Riby, to which estate he had recently succeeded, and on this particular morning our host and I were going out hunting. I well remember the bishop's delight in seeing our host in boots and breeches reading prayers for the household. The appearance of the young man, full of health and vigour, starting the day with public prayer appealed strongly to him, and he frankly showed his pleasure.

"I have mentioned his interest in fox-hunting

because it happened to come under my observation, but he was equally at home with other sportsmen. Ask the shooting-man, and he will tell you of the keenness with which he discussed the day's bag, and the evident delight with which he conversed on the subject. The fact was he had an intense love for the country. Mr. G. W. E. Russell has well shown in his delightful work his interest for birds and flowers, but the whole of nature in the countryside appealed to him. He always appeared intensely happy in the country, and the quieter the surroundings the better pleased he appeared to be. He was quite happy addressing the lads in the churchyard of a village in the midst of nature and in language which they could well understand.

"Nobody can doubt that from the day of his entering the diocese this saintly man was an influence for good in the lives of all with whom he came in contact, no matter what they called themselves as religionists and to what class they belonged. Above all, he was a great gentleman: the courtesy and gentleness of his manner, the sympathy expressed in every line of his features, acted like a magnet, and won at once the confidence of every man or woman who was fortunate enough to meet him.

"Among the impressions his life and character made on the laity in his diocese, I would mention first his intense humility—surely there was never a finer example of a virtue, none too common in the present day, than was shown by this distinguished man in his saintly life and conversation. Mr. Russell has given us the story of his deep interest in visiting the poor young fisherman of Grimsby who was sentenced to death for the murder of his sweetheart. When the death penalty had been exacted the bishop writes to his old friend Mr. Russell, as recorded in his book, not taking any credit to himself for what he had done to save the poor lad's soul. On the contrary he tells him 'it was a terrible privilege; but I am most thankful I was allowed to be with the poor, dear man. He was most beautiful, and his last (and first) communion on Sunday put me to shame. *I felt quite unworthy of him.*' What an example of humility!

"After his humility I would mention his intense human sympathy; he abounded in it, it was evident in every line of his face. Then his simplicity—the simplest incidents in life were sufficient for him, and, as I have stated, he was able to found on them the finest principles and the most necessary lessons. Again, the breadth of his mind and the interest he took, and genuinely felt, in the interests and occupations of others. All these gave him the power of friendship with his hearer, who was made to feel at once that he was speaking not only to a learned divine but to a real friend. The way he expressed himself, the tenderness with which he put his hand on a little boy and blessed him, as he did when my sons were small—all this was done with so much real love and sincerity that it can never be forgotten.

"It must not be inferred that with his tender nature there was any weakness in his character. Though his features were of delicate refinement, the mouth was firm and the chin well-developed. I don't think any one would care to have taken a liberty with him or laid himself open to a rebuke from him. Nobody who ever had the good fortune to meet this saintly man could ever forget his kindly smile, which lit up his whole face. I suppose to reproduce this smile, at once so full of refinement and sympathy and tenderness, in clay would be wellnigh impossible; but, in my judgement, Sir William Richmond has gone as near to doing so as can be expected in the fine statue which records his memory in the minster.

"Bishop King was always glad to be in the company of young men, and his hospitality at the Old Palace was well known. When I commanded the Lincolnshire Yeomanry on one occasion we were camped in Riseholme Park, just outside Lincoln, for our training. The bishop invited the officers to dine with him one evening, and I remember there was some speculation as to whether there would be smoking after dinner, knowing as we did that he himself did not indulge in tobacco; and that smoking was only permitted, as was natural, in a small room downstairs. Knowing his thoughtfulness and hospitality we should not have doubted: after dinner cigarettes were handed round, and, needless to say, we spent a very enjoyable evening.

"The Bishop of Grantham has told me how, on the occasion of another dinner given to Yeomanry officers, with his usual thoughtfulness Bishop King had instructed his chaplain specially to invite his suffragan to dine on this particular evening because he knew his propensities for tobacco, and thought that the officers would be placed more at their ease if they saw the Bishop of Grantham indulging in a cigarette after dinner!"

Holidays

Canon Wilgress, Rector of Great Elm, Somerset, who was the bishop's private chaplain for fifteen years, writes:—

"No one can claim to have really known Bishop King unless he had had the privilege of spending a holiday with him. One of the things which attracted persons to him, wittingly or unwittingly, was the holiday aspect he could throw over so many duties. Holidays were a very real thing to him. Perhaps he never let the outer world so much into his innermost feelings about them as he did in a speech that he made at a prize-giving at the Lincoln Training College, which was held shortly before his last holiday but one; the thought of his holiday was then vividly in his mind, and filled him with overflowing spirits, and enabled him to throw himself with full sympathy into the feelings of the students who were so soon to begin their holidays. The height of hilariousness which his spirits reached on that occasion came as a great surprise to many.

"The thought of his holiday began to take shape some weeks before the actual event. . . . He prepared for it and planned out his tour. If he had no special place he was desirous of seeing, one would be put into his mind sometimes by a friend. This was the case, for example in regard to his resolve to go to Ravenna, which he had long wished to see, and to which he was finally encouraged to go by Bishop Stubbs, who assured him that with reasonable caution it would not be too hot in August.

"If he was sometimes rather slow in making up his mind where to go, when once made he carried out his plan with great inflexibility of purpose. His plan at times was criticized by the cautious as being rash, but his sportsmanlike character would not listen to any such advice. What he had planned he determined to carry out.

"But, combined with the lightheartedness which so characterized his holidays, there was always an element of seriousness; and underlying his plan there were some real principles or objects to be kept in view and attained. There was always a threefold end to be kept in view—physical, mental, and moral.

"It is not necessary to dwell on the first of these, for it is obvious. He carried out the second in a variety of ways. He carefully selected the books he took away with him. There would always be some book of the Bible to read; latterly he used to take a little Hebrew Psalter with Dr. Kay's *Commentary*—a book which he valued very highly. He also generally took the *Paradiso*. He would then add some theological book which had recently been published, and some book on the places he was going to visit (it was the *Life of Theodoric* when he went to Ravenna), or some book on European History. Finally he might take some book likely to give him suggestions for the coming Confirmation tour.

"With regard to the moral end, it will be enough to say that he thought a holiday should always lead on to throwing oneself with increasing zest and determination into the work awaiting one on one's return home.

"On one occasion he copied out and gave to each of his companions the words of

St. Anselm, which he considered summed up the true end of a holiday :—

"'Da mihi quietem et salutem corporis et animae, simulque opportunam ad Te vacationem.' [1]

"He delighted to be able to talk a foreign language ; he could talk French, German, and Italian quite easily ; and in a Catholic country he tried to glean all the information he could about the state of religion in the towns and villages. For this purpose he would call on the curé and try to elicit information from him. His conversations, for the most part, on these occasions, dealt with three points—(1) the state of religion generally ; (2) the possibilities of religious education in the schools of the country ; (3) the supply and training of the clergy. From the curé he often got several Lent Pastoral Letters issued by the bishop of the diocese.

"Sometimes he had the opportunity of getting the information which he desired from the bishop himself, when he happened to get an interview with him.

"Quite a long list might be made of the

[1] Give me rest and health of body and spirit, and at the same time leisure spent agreeably to Thee.

At Tre Croci, near Cortina, 1897.

(From photo by Mrs. T. M. Kitchin.)

Page 216.

foreign bishops with whom he had such interviews. Among these in France were the Archbishop of Rheims and the Bishop of Amiens; and in Italy the Archbishops of Milan, Siena, Brescia, and Verona, and the Bishops of Como and Cremona. He was most anxious to see the Bishop of Cremona, many of whose writings he had read, and indeed he went to Cremona with the special object of seeing him. When he got to the palace he learnt that the bishop was in bed with the gout, but he nevertheless welcomed him in his bedroom, where he sat and talked for some time.

"If he was staying at any place where there were Old Catholics, as for example at Munich, or Zurich, or Bonn, he would try and find out the bishop or leading priests. He felt great sympathy for the Old Catholics, and at times expressed a doubt whether he had done his part by them. He took in regularly one of their periodicals called the *Deutscher Merkur*.

"It would be difficult to say which of the two—Switzerland or Italy—he liked most. Perhaps it would be truer to say that he liked each best in its own way. He immensely enjoyed the strength and grandeur of the Swiss mountains; he felt braced by the invigorating air, and appreciated the strength of the Swiss character. On the other hand, he thoroughly enjoyed the softness of the Italian colouring and the warm and soothing effect of the climate. Latterly he was more inclined to go to Italy, partly because he could see more with less physical fatigue, and partly to get thoroughly baked in the Italian sun after the cold he had experienced during the spring Confirmation tour, and to prepare for the cold of the autumn and winter travelling."

Mrs Kitchin, with her husband the late Mr. T. M. Kitchin, often went abroad, especially to Switzerland, with the bishop. She writes:—

"From the day the blue line was drawn in the bishop's diary, which was done as soon as Easter Day was over, the line showing that all being well the holiday would begin at that date, the bishop in the midst of all his work looked forward with intense delight to the few weeks he hoped to spend in Switzerland and Italy. Writing once he said he was getting into that grumbling and ill-tempered state, which seems to be a necessary preliminary to a holiday! Our holidays with him were spent in Switzerland,

Dr. King, with Canon Wilgress, Mr. Kitchin, and Archdeacon Bond, above Cortina, August, 1896.

Page 218.

we were never with him in Italy. The first time we had the great privilege of travelling with him was in August, 1890. The bishop was then staying at Glion, above Montreux, alone, and he asked us to go on with him to Orleans and Chartres. I remember one little incident of his stay at Glion. A man in the hotel there had broken his collar-bone. When the bishop heard he had been taken to the Infirmary at Montreux, that he had no one with him, he at once went down to visit him. It was on the journey from Orleans to Chartres that I read in *Galignani* of the death of Canon Liddon. I knew what grief this would cause, and hesitated to tell him; but he saw something was wrong, and asked for the paper. I noticed as soon as he caught sight of the name he took off his hat while he read the account. He would not, however, allow his sorrow to interfere with our plans; he went on to Chartres, saw over the cathedral, and in the evening we went to a big fair then being held in the town—he always so much enjoyed mixing with the country people, talking to them, buying "fairings" for the children—it was no unusual sight to see a little child slip its hand into the bishop's and walk beside him.

"On reaching a town of any size where there was a seminary the bishop always went to see the principal and have a talk with him over the religious state of the country. He generally returned from these visits rather depressed, as he had gathered that "indifference," not real hostility as to religion, was the difficulty the priests had to contend with.

"The thoughts that seemed uppermost in his mind during the holiday were always the same. What was the feeling of the people with regard to religion and religious education—he seized every opportunity of asking men he met their opinion on the subject; he was much struck by the way the peasants brought God into their daily lives and work; he delighted to see the women at Evolena going into church before they started work, leaving their scythes in the church porch, and kneeling for a few minutes before the altar. Evolena is a village off the Rhone Valley, to which he was very attached. We were with him there on three separate occasions, as it combined the four things he considered necessary for the right enjoyment of a holiday in Switzerland. It must be a Catholic canton, the hotel must be a fairly comfortable one, there must be a village, and it must be about 5,000 feet up. It was the village life he delighted in; he liked to see the people at work, to talk to them, and to join with them in the service at the parish church; he would speak of their out-of-the-world life. Not that we ought to run away from where we are placed, but, he would add, we lose a great deal in losing simplicity.

"It was the bishop's practice after celebrating the Holy Communion in his own room (if there was no celebration in the hotel) to go to the sung Mass in the village church. It was a great delight to him to spend Sunday in a village, and he would sit out and watch the peasants coming down from the mountains, the wife on a mule carrying a baby, and the husband walking by the side; it reminded him, he would say, of the Blessed Virgin with the Child, and St. Joseph. We want to see more of that in England—husband, wife, and children all going as a duty to worship God. Once he wrote, after a Swiss holiday, 'I do hope there is some real Evolena-like progress in the Church of England—that spirit of restful, dignified contentment which ought to mark all true Church people.' At Saas Fèe we used to have as a guide the village schoolmaster, Ambrose, with whose character he was much struck, saying once of him, 'Ambrose was most beautiful; what chance one has of getting into heaven if that is the sort of standard I can't think—he seemed to have such a nice, simple, sensible mind, and to appreciate any higher kind of remark; it was quite a privilege to be with him.' In speaking of another guide he had at Montana, and a photograph I took of him, he said, 'X. B., with his toes turning in and his hands sprawling, what a wonderful concealment of such a soul!' X. was preparing to be a priest.

"One of the great pleasures of the holiday to the bishop was the flowers; he was a keen botanist, and lover of flowers, especially of the Alpine ones, and would draw your attention to their delicacy and fragility. At Evolena when he was looking at a patch of saxifrage growing on a rock, he quoted from Dr. Moberly's book, *Sorrow, Sin, and Beauty*, and said it lay in us to be beautiful, far transcending the lily.

"Sometimes the bishop would talk about his work in the Diocese, preaching, etc. He thought the foreign priests were often

At Heiligenkreuz, Binn, 1898.

(From a photo by Mrs. T. M. Kitchin.)

Page 222.

more practical in their sermons than ours—they told their people straight out what they were to do. Once he said he did not often compose fresh sermons, but he had one lantern and put in fresh slides. Speaking of a great preacher who had lately died, he said, 'Why was he taken, and we, the dross of the earth, left?'

"In speaking and writing of the holidays, when they were over, the bishop would say that all the great pleasure of the holiday is bound up with Church principles, and all the joy is part of the enjoyment of the Communion of Saints, which gives a restful kind of background to it all."

We venture to add the following characteristic letter, written from Venice during his last visit to Italy, less than two years before he died, to his footman, Herbert Cotgrove, who was engaged to be married. The date is August 8, 1908.

The bishop begins by telling where to send his letters, and then continues:—

"We got here on Friday, after rather a hot week travelling about, after we came down from Abetone. That was a very nice, cool place; this is hot and relaxing, but very curious and interesting. There are no regular streets for carriages, but you go about in funny-looking boats, which they call gondolas, with one or two men to row. They stand up all the time and push their oar before them ; it is a long sort of paddle. They do it wonderfully well. Since I was here (fifty-five years ago !) they have introduced steamboats and all sorts of electric-launches, which rather spoil the place and make it like London with the motor-cars ! but not quite so bad. The wonder is how the houses stand, as they are all built on piles, and some are beautiful palaces.

"It is rather hot and very relaxing. I hope you have had some holiday, and ——[1] too, so as to get ready for the winter work. I should be so glad if you could be settled. The only thing I can do is to encourage you to keep steady, and then, some day, one feels something must come. Remember me to all at the Old Palace.

"God bless you and take care of you.

"Believe me,

"Yours affectionately,

"E. LINCOLN.

"We are all well, thank God."

[1] Cotgrove's *fiancée*.

The late Mr. Frederick Rogers, a well-known Labour Leader, wrote :—

" I was the guest of Bishop King, and had taken part with him the night before in a very different ceremony, for we had sat side by side on the stage of a public hall. Churchmen most of them probably, though I knew some there, old trade-union friends, who were not. It was just a public meeting of quite the ordinary type, and I was curious to see how my host would comport himself as chairman thereof. To me he was one of the most potent spiritual forces of the Church, and his life was an answer, and an entirely convincing one, to a question asked sometimes by our Roman brethren, 'Can your Church produce saints ?' But I knew full well that a saint, by reason of his virtues, might quite easily be a failure at a public meeting ; and my experience had taught me that an excellent man could be the reverse of an excellent chairman.

" But Bishop King, caring nothing—perhaps knowing nothing—of the arts of the platform, by sheer simplicity and sincerity kept his audience in perfect control. It was less a bishop speaking to his diocese than a man speaking to men of the glory and the mystery and the shadows and dark places of life. Now and then it seemed as though a wistful note came into his voice, for he knew their life and his were not the same. But he knew too that for every man, be his place in this struggling and dusty old world what it may, the faith of Christ brought strength and healing to every weakness and disease of the soul; and the chairman's short speech, with its little touches and suggestions of the spiritual side of things, was an eminently practical one, illustrating an old truth, familiar to every student of psychology, that the most profound mystic is often the most practical man.

"Bishops are persons of limited leisure, and are not always able to command the graces and the charms of conversation as Mandell Creighton could. Two things impressed me in my brief talks with Bishop King: his wonderful humility and his high intellectual integrity. He and I were at opposite points of the compass in many things, and he must have differed profoundly from much that fell from my lips. But the gentle criticism and shrewd, sound wisdom of his words brought with them a wonderful charm; and the poet's phrase, 'clear dream and solemn vision,' was constantly recurring to me as I saw from many standpoints his transparent and lofty mind. The *Times* found that the position he held in the English Church 'was due to qualities rather of the heart than of the head; it was involved in the intrinsic attractiveness of the man much more than in the intellectual power of the teacher.' The statement may pass; but its truth depends a good deal on what the *Times* means by 'intellectual power.' There was a fine intellectual power in Bishop King, but it was applied to themes not discussed in newspapers.

"The qualities of the heart were there in overflowing abundance. Honoured by scholars and beloved of undergraduates in Oxford, he won too the affection of grooms and stable-boys by his simple and direct utterances, touched as they often were with Apostolic fervour. There is little enough of idealism in working-class lads; the whole tendency of modern civilization is to destroy it, and not many men, as years grow upon them, can keep their natures fresh enough to win the sympathy of youth. But Bishop King did not appear to be touched by the mental stiffening that time so often brings, and those who would seek the explanation should read carefully his *Lectures to Men*, or *Meditations on the Last Seven Words*.

"Those who fear that the things of the soul will be ultimately submerged in the welter of pleasure-seeking and materialistic ideals that is around us to-day may find an answer to their forebodings in a life like that of Bishop King. Always regarded as an extreme man, he nevertheless united all parties in a wonderful way, and was beloved as much by the Evangelicals as by the extreme men of his own school. And this was as it should be, for truth and reality were his only aims. A Congregational minister of his diocese, the Rev. George Barrett, wrote of him : 'His beautiful spirit, his Christ-like character, his intense loyalty to conviction and to His Church, have won the respect of all sections of the community, and have enriched the Christian life of the city.' A trade unionist wrote to me : 'I was in Lincoln when the bishop passed away. The whole of the city was moved. Everybody seemed affected.' 'A saintly man' was the general description."

CHAPTER X

THE BISHOP'S MESSAGE

Ma chi prende sua croce e segue Cristo,
Ancor mi scuserà di quel ch' io lasso,
Vedendo in quell' albor balenar Cristo.

Par. xiv. 106–8.

But whoso takes his cross, and follows Christ,
Will pardon me for that I leave untold,
When in the fleckered dawning he shall spy
The glitterance of Christ.

Cary.

CHAPTER X

THE BISHOP'S MESSAGE

WE may now pass on to consider more in detail Bishop King's faith and teaching. Two well-known sayings give the best summary of his message. One has already been quoted from his primary charge "To bring home to the people, and especially to the poor, the blessings of the Church"; the other often occurs in his writings, and is best known in the form it takes in the letter he wrote to the diocese only a few days before his death: "My great wish has been to lead you to be Christ-like Christians." They are not chance utterances. They are continually found in sermons and pastoral letters during the whole of his Episcopate.

THE CHURCH

His teachings on the Church are perfectly clear and definite, but there is an almost entire absence of any controversial tone. The letter to the Rev. C. J. Elliott in answer to the attack made upon the teachings and devotions at Cuddesdon is proof enough that he could have made a powerful use of criticism and argument in matters of controversy had he chosen to do so. It has an argumentative force, an intellectual clearness, an underlying current of irony, a sense of outraged justice, a ruthless logic in pinning his opponent down to unsubstantiated statements. It reminds one at times of William Law's letter to Hoadly, or of Dr. Liddon in one of those moods of refined irony he could at times use with such astonishing effect. It is the only example of such method in Bishop King's writings, and it dates from before the Episcopate. Apart from its real worth as a testimony to the bishop's doctrinal convictions in the matters of Penitence and the Holy Eucharist, it has a special value in showing that he possessed controversial powers of which he might have made frequent use, but that he deliberately chose to keep them in reserve and to adopt a gentler, and, probably in the long run, a more effectual method of ministerial teaching. In the avoidance of controversy he never shunned definite teaching of the Faith, but he rather set it forth as an intense personal

Ap: 23. 1900

My Dearest Child

We shall be delighted to see you tomorrow, any time you please.

I am so glad & thankful ~~that~~ — your dear Father is better. My love & sympathy to them. My love & blessing to you

yours ever aff

E. Lincoln

Autograph Letter to Rev. B. W. Randolph.

Page 232.

conviction which he assumed people held with him, than as a position he was endeavouring to prove. He expounded it. He explained and illustrated it. He set forth its interest, its beauty, its wonder, its force, its power. He made clear its appeal, not to the intellect only, but to the whole nature, and especially to the conscience, of his hearers. His method was that described by St. Paul—"By manifestation of the truth, commending ourselves to every man's conscience in the sight of God."

In his doctrinal statements on the Church his sermons abound in references to the experience he could take for granted in the simplest people, that the individual can only find perfection in the community, in the family, in the State, in the Church as the Body of Christ. He never tired of illustrations manifesting the truth that in every sphere of life God uses material things for the conveyance of His blessings, intellectual, moral, social, spiritual. His great and noteworthy teaching, already referred to in the account of his primary charge, as to the meaning and danger of impatience under the disciplinary methods of the mediatorial kingdom of our Lord, soon became familiar to well-instructed

Church people in the diocese. He continually urged the study of Church history, and often showed by striking instances that it is not simply a matter of names and dates and controversies, but a large and delightful and glorious revelation of divine power and life in great epochs of human history and in individual souls. Probably, however, as his Pastoral Letters witness, he believed the practical working of the Church's methods and sacraments and devotions to be the most effectual means of bringing home the blessings of the Church to the people of the diocese.

"The Church is the Body of Christ, in which individual members are meant to find their perfection."

"It ought to thrill the hearts of real Churchmen to realize the vastness of the Body of Christ extending on and on all over the earth."

"The continuity of the Church rests on the presence of our Lord in the lives of its members."

"We are members of a divinely-founded and indestructible society, but we belong at present to that Church in her militant condition."

"It is almost impossible to overestimate the

secret influence of the Church on the growth of our English constitution and on the character of the people. It is the lawful pride of the Church of England that she is not afraid of historical or any other form of truth."

"A great remedy against despondency through isolation is to be found in a brighter faith that the Head of the Church is watching the works of His people."

"The true work of the Church is to bring men to that perfection it is intended they should reach in holiness and holy living."

PERSONALITY

His message was his own experience of the faith and religion of Jesus Christ. It was always this. It was always perfectly clear, distinct, accurate; but it was the truth as it had been brought home to him in the experiences of his long life and his dealings with souls. It was the Church's Faith, but it had the colour and warmth of his own personal experience. It is always so with the greatest teachers. It is the secret of their spiritual power. Such men do not simply set forth the facts of revelation and the methods of divine grace. They manifest its power. "While

I was thus musing the fire kindled ; and at the last I spake with my tongue."

One of the bishop's deepest convictions was an abiding sense of the reality of human personality and all that it involves. He spoke continually of the great contribution the Oxford teachers of the sixties and seventies, especially Professor T. H. Green, had made to his spiritual life and knowledge. It would almost seem that he put in the first place this recovery (as he termed it) of belief in human personality.

"Men were raised up to help us, and we regained the conviction of the reality of our own personality. The '*I* am *I*, and I know it,' became a fact full of priceless power and hope. Moral phenomena became our facts as sure as those of any other science ; we learnt not to be ashamed to say we did not know all. Others were getting to know enough to see that they could not explain everything. There were found to be mysteries on both sides, and it was not thought unscientific to admit it. Our personality we might not be able satisfactorily to define, but we were sure of its reality ; and inseparable from it we found reason and will and love. We saw a difference between right and wrong quite different from the difference of colours ; a difference which caused an attraction or a revulsion to our whole being.

"We felt we were *free*—free to do right, and free to do wrong. We could do either, but we knew we *ought* to do right ; our feet stood again on the divine pathway of *duty*. We saw the exceeding excellence of moral beauty in others quite apart from wealth, or rank, or intellect ; we saw it in the poor, we felt the thrill of it in ourselves.

"And, from the recovered vantage-ground of the divine pathway, we were led to look upward, and we received new assurances to our belief in a personal God—not as a mere intellectual conclusion, but as the outcome of our entire personality acting as a whole—our reason, our affections, our will ; we realized afresh the necessity of offering ourselves, our souls, and bodies as a complete burnt-offering to God. We felt that we could not afford, so to say, to let go our hold on God by any one part of our nature ; God had so distributed the evidences of Himself to our whole being that our duty towards God was evidently to believe in Him, to fear Him, and to love Him with all our *heart*, all our *mind*, all our *soul*, all our *strength*." [1]

The reality of human personality was a constant subject in his sermons. It was one of the grounds of his faith in the value of the individual life. People were never in his sight merely "hands" or "workers" or means; always persons with special powers and gifts and capacities. Those gifts might be latent. He seemed to see us as we are meant to be, as we perhaps really are, rather than as we appear on the surface. It was one of the secrets of his sympathy. It was the lesson he had learnt, not only from the Oxford of his own time but from Bishop Butler, whose *Analogy* and *Charge to the Clergy of the Diocese of Durham* were his constant companions. In all his ethical teachings it might almost be said he had, as a friend has put it, "always in view the powers and capacities of those to whom he was speaking, and with whom he dealt, rather than any high and hard and arbitrary laws and principles."

And this intense belief in the value and reality of human personality was one source,

[1] Address to members of the Lambeth Conference—*Love and Wisdom of God*, pp. 307, 308.

at any rate, of the strength and firmness of his will and purpose. People sometimes fancied he was too full of tenderness and sympathy to be strong; but those who ever tried to move him from some conviction or line of action knew better. He was himself. He had his own experiences. He would have to give a personal account for them. He was troubled to find himself at variance with others. "He could no other"; but it was not his fault if there was any breach of friendship.

For example, there was one subject upon which he felt compelled to take an independent line, although it gave much pain and sorrow to some of his best friends—the question which arose as to the absolute indissolubility of marriage. He had no uncertainty as to "what is God's original antecedent will with regard to marriage; of that there can be no doubt." But he urged that "the point of view from which we should consider this question is not ideal, but practical, ethical, remedial . . . to see what may be done under the head of equity and mercy." He dealt fully with the question in his charge in 1895; and he arrived at the conclusion that the general principle laid down in St. Mark and St. Luke should be regarded as limited by the one exception specified in St. Matthew; and he was convinced "in looking back over the chief sources of evidence, over councils, penitential books, the early fathers, the later history of the Church," that statements and hesitations were found which "would not have been possible if the absolute indissolubility of marriage under all circumstances had been the accepted traditionary teaching of the Church." He therefore accepted the statement of the Lambeth Conference of 1888:—"The Conference recommends that the Clergy should not be instructed to refuse the Sacraments or other privileges of the Church to those who under civil sanction are thus married," i.e. in the case of the "innocent party" having contracted another union.

The Lincoln trial has not been dealt with in any detail in this volume. Those who wish for a full account will find it in Mr. Russell's book; but it illustrates the present point of view. The controversy was thrust upon the bishop. It was a real trouble to him, an interference with his work; but he never hesitated for a moment. He knew what he wanted. He knew he was right. He realized the issues involved. He went right through. "He could no other."

All this may seem to be overlabouring the point, but it is of primary value if the bishop's character is to be understood. It gave him his intense pastoral love, his care for human souls. Each one he had to do with was a special creation of Almighty GOD; the object of divine love of such value that it could only be redeemed by the Precious Blood; a separate individual being, a personal soul. And it gave a breadth to his outlook on human life and thought. No one ever accused him of narrowness. His intense belief in human personality made him realize the distinctions and differences that are found in human lives and characters.

A SUMMARY OF FAITH

In the addresses at the Lambeth Conference he speaks very insistently of what he calls the value of mental exercise upon the principal points of the Faith. It was his own continual practice. He found it useful, not only in deepening his own knowledge of the separate parts of the Faith, but in enabling him to see their relations as a whole and the limits of our knowledge in such matters. He had found people frightened at themselves, fearing they were falling into unbelief, when the simple truth was "they had never accustomed themselves to think out what they believed." It was one of his constant teachings.

"From the want of sufficient thought on the great truths of religion our lives are in danger of losing that brilliancy and perfection which the light of truth would naturally give."

"Too many of us hold the Christian Religion with the tips of our intellectual fingers, instead of embracing it with our whole heart."

Here is what he said on the subject in one of his addresses during the quiet day at Lambeth :—

"I have seemed to find a real and helpful sequence of thought in these seven words—'Duty,' 'Conscience,' 'God,' 'Scripture,' 'Christ,' 'Church,' 'Holy Spirit'; and I have found it useful to myself to exercise myself on these words, and I have suggested them to others, cautioning them to beware of thinking that they can do their duty without recognizing the claims of conscience; and to beware of thinking that they will be able to keep their conscience as it ought to be unless they acknowledge God; and to beware lest they lose their hold on God without the aid of His own revelation—the Bible; to beware of thinking that they believe the Bible unless they believe in Christ; to beware of thinking that they can partake of Christ with all the fullness that may be theirs, except in the way He has appointed, through His Church; and, finally, to beware of thinking that they can do all these things in their natural strength, without accepting the gift of the Spirit.

"And so again, I have found it useful, in some cases, to suggest the consideration of these words in the inverse order. To caution some persons against thinking that they are living in the Spirit unless they are willing to be guided by the Church. To caution some to beware of trusting to their zeal for the Church unless they really look to Christ, to the example of His life, the reality of forgiveness through the atoning power of His death, and the power of His Resurrection; to beware of thinking that they will be able to keep their hold on Christ unless they search the Scriptures with the view of coming nearer to Him, of growing in grace and in the knowledge of our Lord and Saviour Jesus Christ; to beware of trusting to a mere knowledge of the Scriptures unless they set God always before them, obeying their conscience as His voice, and showing their obedience by doing their daily duty, however humble it may be. Some simple considerations of this kind, such as any poor person might understand, might be found to preserve a living relation to the truth, and to give unity and power to the life." [1]

And those last words were perfectly sincere. He often made those "words" and their relation one to another the subjects of a sermon. He used them as almost a rule of faith in the Diocesan Guilds Manual. And the notes—fairly full notes—still exist of the addresses upon them given to the servants at family prayers in the palace chapel.

FAITH IN GOD

The bishop's sermons and teachings might almost be read as an exposition of these great

[1] *Love and Wisdom of God*, pp. 313, 314.

fundamental truths. Only one or two examples can be taken. Here is one, setting forth what he realized and meant by faith in God:—

"Personal devotedness to a Personal God is one of the chief marks of a true religion. The Bible calls it walking before the face of God, walking with God. Christianity, in its essential working, is not a religion of detachment, but of attachment; a religion not of fear, but of love. It is the assurance of the companionship of a Friend always able and willing to guide, check, and support us in all dangers; a Friend whose rod and staff will still be with us, guiding, protecting, even through the valley of the shadow of death; a Friend whose constant companionship ought to lift up our fallen countenance, and give us, even now, on the journey of life, a brightness that should witness to those who meet us of the reality of the companionship we enjoy. All this is no mere language of theoretical theology, or excited devotional feeling, but may be the sure experience of your daily lives.

"A singular sense of security, a peculiar independence of place and time, a secret satisfaction, a quiet courage, an inward peace, an increasing hope, a purer, truer, and more extending love—these are some of the well-known proofs of the reality of our personal relation with God, and of His companionship with us." [1]

"A consciousness of His presence and His love." It was a life-long experience, a life-long prayer. It became almost a form of personal blessing. It was his last message to his diocese, as it was, not seldom, the last word, especially in letters to friends—"May God guide and bless you and refresh you with the increasing consciousness of His presence and His love."

THE SAVIOUR

"He preached Christ to them." This might well be the motto of all Bishop King's sermons. The two chief aspects of his preaching were the Saviour's Death and the Saviour's Power in the realm of grace. It is significant that he nearly always speaks of our Lord as the "Saviour." There are perhaps only two of all his published sermons in which the name does not occur; and there are only two or three, and those rather discourses on special occasions than sermons, in which there

[1] *Love and Wisdom of God*, p. 46.

are not direct references to the Saviour's Death upon the Cross for the salvation of souls. They are never brought in simply for the sake of bringing them in ; there is no feeling as we read the words that the reference was made of direct purpose with the idea that a sermon could not be a Gospel sermon without it. It occurs quite simply, quite naturally. It was one of his own most familiar experiences. He had known the power of the Cross. He had been forgiven. He had seen the same experience in countless souls. It was as simple, as elemental, as fundamental as any experience of life and love and humanity. It was always somewhere about his mind, and of course it came up when he was writing or speaking about the deepest things of life. There was no rhetoric, no rhapsody ; always a deep, grave, wondering earnestness, which made a sentence, even a phrase, stand out in startling reality in the midst of the words of one who was more real and measured in his preaching than most men of his generation.

With all his sympathy and hopefulness, he was under no misapprehension about the sin and wickedness in the world. You had only to look at him when he was speaking of it to see his sense of the seriousness, of the gravity, of the misery, of the sinfulness of sin. He seems to have regarded it chiefly from the point of view of the ruin it had wrought from the beginning and was still working in human nature. The Cross was its only remedy. The world needs the Cross absolutely as much to-day as two thousand years ago. "We are made in the image and likeness of God, and Christ came to restore that image and likeness." "Through the means of Grace we see the possibility of that restoration of the image of God in man which we believe the Saviour came down from heaven to restore." Amongst those means of grace the bishop had an intense belief in the benefit of Absolution. It was a constant blessing in his own life and a continual part of his ministry to souls. "Penitents find peace at the foot of the Cross; it is like the birth of a rose out of the winter bough."

Enough has, perhaps, been said about the bishop's sacramental teaching. He believed with all his heart and soul that the blessings won for us by the Incarnation and Redemption are conveyed to us in and by the sacraments. Baptism, Confirmation, Absolution, and Holy

Communion—these are all means of grace which join us to the God-united humanity of Jesus Christ. His own life was an abiding illustration of his faith.

"Let us strive to realize," he says, "in as true proportion as we can the fullness of the Eucharistic Mystery—the Sacrifice, the Communion, the Worship." And again, "The ineffable Presence of the Saviour in the Holy Eucharist is meant to go with us and be with us in our daily life."

THE CHRIST-LIKE LIFE

"He preached Christ unto them." And his message was more and more as the years went on the possibility of the Christ-like life. It had always been this, but in later years it grew more insistent. It was seldom set forth in detail. He dwelt, of course, again and again upon the Saviour's life as being the perfect pattern for us to follow, but it was always the "Saviour's" life. It was not only that he taught men to copy the details of the earthly life of our Lord, but rather he made men realize that the life of union with Christ in faith and prayer and sacrament must issue in a Christ-like life if it has any reality at all.

It is His life within us. "My great wish has been to lead you to be Christ-like Christians. In Christ is the only hope of purity and peace. In Him we may be united to God and to one another." These were his last words to the diocese, and they gather up his whole teaching—that we are called "to love God and to love one another in God." If humanity ever realizes and lives it out here on earth, all our sorrows and troubles and problems will pass for ever.

"We know now what value God puts on man since Christ has come down to save him."

"The Blood of Christ can cleanse our human life from the sins of passion and indulgence."

"Our Saviour's example must be the true pattern for us to follow, however hard it may be for fallen man to apply it to himself."

"We need to reconsider our conception of the capabilities of man by the example of Christ."

"The victory of the grace of Christ is part of the evidence we should contribute in these days to the truth and power of Christianity."

"We must never allow it to be said that the grace of Christ is unequal to that which He said it would do."

"The realization of the Life of Christ as a new moral force in humanity fills us with inspiration and hope."

"Christ has become to His people not a far-off Name, but the sum of many satisfactions."

"We shall have reached the true end of this life of discipline when we have gained love of God and love of man."

"This is the ultimate and ennobling idea to set before ourselves—the unity of man in communion with God."

SOCIAL WELFARE

In politics and social questions the bishop was satisfied to enunciate great principles rather than to undertake any active work for their immediate application. He was a bishop first, not a politican or a social reformer. And yet he had a keen interest in all the questions of the day. More than once when his visit to some great house where politics had an absorbing interest was anticipated with a slightly amused hesitation by his hosts it was found, to their great relief, that he was quite as much up in the great political question of the day as they were ; especially was this the case in one instance with reference to what then seemed the somewhat extreme Budget proposals of the year. His faith in humanity kept him free from any fear of crisis. He had too keen an outlook, and he understood human life too well to be always an optimist, but he was always hopeful. A disciple of Dante, he had some measure of his austerity and tenderness, but an even larger share of his hopefulness. It runs like a ray of sunshine through all his life, his teachings, his experiences, his sermons. It might almost be said of him through his long eighty years—

> [1] "La chiesa militante alcun figliuolo
> Non ha con più speranza."
> *Par.* xxv. 52–3.

He was an Englishman with a deep patriotism and loyalty, a real belief in the value of conduct and goodness in daily life, with an Englishman's temperament and outlook, and all that this involves in religion and social life—a love of freedom, a love of justice, a fearless courage, and a quiet, religious sense. But how far had he realized the new England, the new questions,

[1] "Among her sons, not one more full of hope
Hath the Church militant." *Cary.*

new criticism, new social problems? He saw them coming. He was too old to have any direct part in their working out, but he laid down quite clearly and distinctly over and over again the great lines on which he felt they must be prepared for and faced. Here are a dozen maxims taken from five times the number on this subject printed in the "Bishop King Kalendar" a year or two after his death. They might almost form the leading principles in a programme of social welfare.

"We cannot reach our individual perfection without fulfilling our duties to others."

"The word 'politics,' sometimes degraded by the selfishness of party spirit, really means the science of the well-being of the community."

"The need of conducting municipal life with a sense of Christian obligation is being brought home to us with increasing reality."

"It is the truest wisdom and prudence in Church or State to acknowledge faults where they exist, and to seek to procure their remedy."

"To fit oneself to take some part in the great organization of national life should be the ennobling ambition of us all."

"It is the strength and glory of England that she offers the highest places in the administration of her power to all who are willing and able to attain them."

"What we want is increased faith in the capabilities of the people; but it has to be got at by slow steps."

"We must not give up any soul as hopeless."

"The housing of the people is in reality intimately connected with the social and moral condition of the nation."

"Much, I hope, will be done to improve the temporal conditions of the people, and I hope for great moral and spiritual results."

"We should acknowledge God in trade by truthfulness of work, by fair dealing, and by fair wages."

"Employers of labour should ask themselves what they are doing for the souls of those they employ."

"There is one law for all; there must be no scamped work, but all must be done as under the eye of God, the Master of us all."

"The triumphs of science bring into greater prominence the triumphant possibilities of man's higher powers."

"We need to put our modern life into more direct and conscious contact with the will of God."

"It is a matter of thankfulness and hope that social and national troubles are leading men to look to Christ as the true solution of our difficulties."

"Perfected humanity will be the full contribution of all those characteristics God has given to the nations of men—lifted up and perfected in Christ."

THE MORAL GOVERNMENT OF GOD

"I believe more and more in the reality and power and awful exactness of the moral government of the world." This was the bishop's ground of confidence and comfort as he looked out at the strange confusions and complexities of life here on earth. It was a frequent subject of his sermons and especially of his missionary addresses.

"The contrast between the certainty of the secret working of God to carry out His own purpose, and the apparent confusion and failure through which this purpose is often brought about, are well worthy of our constant remembrance. As we look back over the history of the world many examples might be given of apparent ruin through which God was working out a higher good. And two such catastrophes stand out above the rest. One was the destruction of the Jewish State and Temple ; the other the breaking up of the Roman Empire. . . . Apparently all seemed to be given over to confusion and ruin, while in reality God was so overruling and guiding as to make all things work together for good to those who would love Him. Such a belief in Providence guiding and governing the nations of the world needs amongst us Christians careful cultivation. We pray that 'the course of this world may be peaceably ordered by God's governance.' Such a prayer is a divine act of faith in God's government of the world."[1]

And the bishop always found the contrast between the apparent failure and collapse and catastrophe of Good Friday and the great victory of Easter Day a reason for the renewal of his trust in the overruling wisdom and love of God. Apparently, all things were most contrary ; in reality, all things were working together for good.

"It is a special feature of the Old Testament

[1] *Easter Sermons*, pp. 69–71.

revelation that God is the Lord and Ruler of the whole world, and not of the chosen people only."

"Study the history of the world to realize more fully the presence and the power of the hand of God under which we live."

"The thought of God's eternal plan and purpose should help to keep us calm and steady at all times."

The Faith had come into his life not merely as a new interest or an intellectual conviction, but as a spiritual power satisfying the deepest needs of his soul. He had seen it embodied in men of great holiness of life. He had lived near enough to the days of the Tractarian Movement to know some of its greatest leaders. He had felt the influence of the movement, with all that was in it of "religious earnestness and aspiration, of self-devotion, affectionateness, and high and refined and varied character, displayed under circumstances which are scarcely intelligible to men of the present time."[1]

He looked back to those men as teachers and friends, to whose words and example he

[1] Dean Church. Letter to Lord Acton, April, 1885.

owed an almost infinite debt. It was through them he had received what he always held to be the "Faith once delivered to the saints, the Faith set forth in Holy Scripture and in the writings of the ancient Fathers of the undivided Church." It had come with the added power of truth that was suffering opposition, even persecution, at the hands of absolute ignorance and obstinate prejudice. He had found its highest and best expositions in the writings of Mr. Keble and Dr. Pusey. He was absolutely satisfied. He always fell back upon their teachings when he needed definite expositions of the Faith. He was always anxious to put his doctrinal statements in words that would have been in exact and perfect harmony with their teaching.

No attempt has been made to touch upon the subject of the bishop's inner and spiritual life of devotion and fellowship with God, but enough has been said in various parts of this book to show its intensity and reality. It was a life "hid with Christ in God." It was a sacramental life, fed daily by the Eucharistic Food. His consciousness of the presence and love of God was the predominant feature of that life; only equalled by his desire that others should share this blessed experience. He seldom, indeed, spoke of his most intimate feelings, but his letters are often lit up with expressions which reveal them; and the joy which showed itself continually and almost uninterruptedly in his life was surely the outcome of the love of God and love of man which was evermore burning within him. But once more his letters reveal the man. "Simplicity, tenderness, sympathy, and love—combined with deep spiritual insight"—are the prevailing notes of all his spiritual letters, while, as has been said, "ever and anon there are flashes of that quiet humour and playfulness which those who knew him will recognize as one of the most delightful and never-failing traits of his beautiful, inspiring, and uplifting character."

MARCH 8, 1910

The record of the last days has been told with great love and tenderness by Canon Wilgress in Mr. Russell's book. His body rests in the cloister garth under the shadow of the great broad tower of the cathedral. None who knew and loved him ever pass by without some thought of his life and all that he was to us.

Others had laboured, and he entered into their labours. He carried on the message and strove to bring it home to the simplest souls in the diocese. He was their "Friend and Bishop," as he loved to sign himself in his Pastoral Letters. He loved the people. And that love was returned a thousandfold, and with that return there grew up what he treasured more—the beginning of a real love for the Church in the hearts of the people, and the endeavour in multitudes of men and women and even children to follow Christ as he followed Him, to live a Christ-like life.

We knew a saint had lived amongst us.

DEO GRATIAS.

Memorial Statue in Lincoln Cathedral.

(From a photo by S. Smith.)

Page 260.

INDEX

Printed by A. R. Mowbray & Co. Ltd.
London and Oxford